QUICKLY AGING HERE

Geof Hewitt, twenty-six, was born and raised in Montclair, New Jersey. Founding editor of The Kumquat Press, he has studied at Cornell University, Johns Hopkins, and the University of Iowa. Two short collections of his poetry have been published: *Poem & Other Poems* (The Kumquat Press), and *Waking Up Still Pickled* (The Lillabulero Press). He is now teaching English at the University of Hawaii.

QUICKLY AGING HERE

Some Poets of the 1970's

EDITED BY GEOF HEWITT

ANCHOR BOOKS

Doubleday & Company, Inc., Garden City, New York

The editor wishes to thank the magazines and publishers who have
given generous permission to reprint the following poems:

Alfred Starr Hamilton's "Anything Remembered," "April Lights," "Guardian,"
"Liquid'll," "Town," "White Chimes," from *Epoch,* © 1963, 1964, 1967
by Cornell University; "Bronze," "Didn't You Ever Search for Another
Star?" "Psyche," from *Sphinx,* © 1968 by The Kumquat Press.

Shirley Kaufman's "I Hear You," "Mothers, Daughters," from *Poetry North-
west,* Spring 1968, © 1968 by Shirley Kaufman; "It Stays," from
The Southern Review, Spring 1969, © 1969 by Shirley Kaufman; "The
Hunger," "Watts," from *Choice,* © 1967 by *Choice,* a Magazine of Poetry
and Photography; "Room" from *New American Review* #2, © 1967 by
Shirley Kaufman.

Eric Torgersen's "Aubade," from *kayak* 13; "I'm Married," "The Cage,"
from *Epoch,* © 1967, 1964 by Cornell University; "jensen: a slideshow,"
from *Poetry Northwest,* Summer 1969, © 1969 by Eric Torgersen; "Leg-
ends," from *Lillabulero* by permission of Lillabulero Press.

Philip Dow's "Death," from *The Nation,* © 1968 by The Nation Associates
Inc.; "The Life of the Poet," "Twilight in California," from *Choice,* ©
1967, 1969.

Joseph Cardarelli's "The Marlborough Poems," "Waiting for Lunch," from
Kumquat 2, © 1968 by The Kumquat Press; "Refrain" (originally en-
titled: "Connection") from *Epoch,* © 1968 by Cornell University.

Coleman Barks's "Body" from *Tennessee Poetry Journal,* © 1968 by Tennessee
Poetry Journal; "Choosing," from *Hiram Poetry Review,* May 1968, ©
1968; "The Driver," from *Foxfire,* March 1968, © 1968 by Eliot Wig-
ginton; "Feather River Valley," from *Latitudes,* © 1969; "Finger of
Necessity," from *Kumquat* 3, © 1969 by The Kumquat Press; "Nickajack
Cave," from *Ann Arbor Review* #5/6, Spring 1969, © 1969 by Fred
Wolven; "The Oracle," from *Gnosis,* Fall 1968, © 1968.

Sophia Castro-Leon's "A Letter," "Again Beginning," "Soft Rain," "Turning,"
from *Kumquat,* © 1967, 1968 by The Kumquat Press; "The Eye,"
"Paces," from *kayak* 11.

Dennis Trudell's "Gambol," "The Jump Shooter," from *The Fiddlehead;* "Going to Pittsburgh," "The Guest," from *The Wormwood Review* #30,
© 1968 by The Wormwood Review.

David Hilton's "Childhood Ambition," "Hang On," from *Kumquat* 3, © 1969
by The Kumquat Press; "Zoo, with Lamp and Chairs,"
from *University of Tampa Poetry Review,* © 1969 by Duane Locke; "The
Newlyweds' Accident," from *Poetry Northwest,* Winter 1967–68, © 1968
by David Hilton; "Sunday Again," from *Abraxas* 1, © 1968 by Abraxas
Press. "In Praise of BIC Pens" from *Chicago Review.*

Mary Ellen Solt's "Lobelia," "Marigold," "Wild Crab," from *Flowers In Concrete*, Design Program, Fine Arts Dept., Indiana U; "Zinnia," from *Concrete Poetry, Britain, Canada, and the U.S.A.;* "The Visitor," from *Poor Old Tired Horse.*

William Hathaway's "Card Burning in Central Park," "Conspiracy in Iowa," from *New: American & Canadian Poetry* #8; © 1968 by John Gill; "When Beulah Did the Hula" from *Poetry Northwest*, Winter 1968–69, © 1969 by William Hathaway.

Joseph Brown, S.J.'s "upon which to rejoice," from *America,* © *America,* National Catholic Weekly, New York, N.Y. 10019.

Thomas Hanna's "I Make Fallout Too," from *Epoch*, Fall, 1968, © 1968 by Cornell University; "The Downtown Swan Thing," from *Latitudes,* © 1969; "Christmas, Ibiza," from *West Coast Review,* © 1969; "The Song of Casyor Brioschi," from *The Trojan Horse.*

Barbara L. Greenberg's "Pan American Flight 207—Delayed," from *The Michigan Quarterly Review VI*, 1967, © 1967 by The University of Michigan; "April 31st," "The Husband," from *Premiere* 4, © 1967; "The Gentleman's Garden," *Poetry Northwest*, Summer, 1969 © 1969 by Barbara L. Greenberg; "Poem for a Dead Aunt," from *The Antioch Review;* "Wedlock," from *Shenandoah,* © 1969 by *Shenandoah*: The Washington and Lee University Review.

Stan Rice's "On the Murder of Martin Luther King," from *Choice,* © 1969 by *Choice.*

Floyce Alexander's "Li Po," from *Voyages;* "Nowhere," from *Choice,* © 1969 by *Choice;* "Poem for a Painter," from *Tri-Quarterly* 12, © 1969 by *Tri-Quarterly* 12, Northwestern University Press; "The Lotus Eaters," from *kayak* 15.

William Witherup's "For Robert Bly," from *Prairie Schooner,* © 1969; "Marian at Tassajara Springs," "The Great White Father," from *Lillabulero* by permission of Lillabulero Press; "On the Death of Theodore Roethke," from *Prairie Schooner,* Spring, 1966, © William Witherup, "Freeway," from *Trace,* © 1969 by James Boyer May.

Sandford Lyne's "Notes from an Ohio Tavern," from *The Plum Creek Review.*

Peter Fellowes's "A Change of Heart," "Predator," from *Epoch*, Spring, 1968, © 1968 by Cornell University; "View from an American Window," from *Kumquat* 1, © 1967 by The Kumquat Press.

Colette Inez's "Cold Waltzes," from *The Nation,* © 1963 by The Nation Associates, Inc.; "For Denise McNair," from *Open Places* 4, © 1968 by *Open Places;* "Force of Snow," from *Shenandoah,* © 1968 by *Shenandoah*: The Washington and Lee University Review; "Sauerkraut Talk Shreds," from *Trace* 66, © 1968 by James Boyer May; "Slumnight," from *Poetry Bag,* © 1968 by *Poetry Bag;* "The Woman Who Loved Worms," from *Four Quarters,* © 1967 by La Salle College; "Unaware that Avessek," from *Latitudes,* © 1969.

William Brown's "An Exchange of Letters," "Minding Our Own Business," from *Poetry Northwest,* © 1968 by William Brown; "Wondering How," from *The North American Review,* © 1967 by Cornell College.

Gerald Butler's "This Side of Orion," [Part I, 'Flash,' from *The Hudson Review*, Vol. XVII, No. 2 (Summer, 1964). © 1964 by The Hudson Review, Inc.]; [Part 12, from *Hollow Orange*]

Dan Gillespie's "Abandoned Copper Refinery," from *Chelsea* 20/21, © 1967 by de Palchi Corporation Publisher; "Desert Gulls," "Poem for the Disappearing Bear," "For a Bum Seen Walking," from *kayak* (10 & 14); "Strip Mining Pit," from *Choice*, © 1969 by *Choice;* "To New Jerusalem," from *The Carleton Miscellany*, © 1967 by Carleton College.

Craig Sterry's "Margaret," from *Pebble* 1, © 1968 by Greg Kuzma; "Montana Visit," from *Lillabulero*, by permission of Lillabulero Press; "Dream Poem №1" from *Wormwood Review*, © 1969 by *The Wormwood Review;* "To a Suicide," from *Southern Poetry Review*, Spring, 1969.

Denis Johnson's "Checking the Traps," "The Man Among the Seals," from *The North American Review*, © 1969 by The University of Northern Iowa; "Quickly Aging Here," from *Sou'Wester*, © 1969 by The Board of Trustees of Southern Illinois University.

NOTE

Since this anthology was edited, several of the poets have had book manuscripts accepted for publication. The list which follows is complete as of September 1969. Dates of publication are only approximate.

Alfred Starr Hamilton: *Selected Poems*; Jargon Books (Highlands, N.C.): 1970.

Shirley Kaufman: *The Floor Keeps Turning* (Winner of the U. S. Award of the International Poetry Forum); University of Pittsburgh Press: January 1970.

    My Little Sister (translations), by Abba Kovner; Penguin Books (New York): 1970.

Eric Torgersen: *The Carpenter*; The Salt Mound Press (Buffalo, N.Y.): 1969.

Coleman Barks: an as yet untitled collection of poems; Harper & Row (New York): 1970.

David Hilton: *The Shot Goes In*; Quixote Press (Madison, Wisc.): 1969.

Mary Ellen Solt: *The Peoplemover: 1968*; The Finial Press (Urbana, Ill.): 1970.

Raymond DiPalma & Stephen Shrader: *Macaroons*; Doones Press (Bowling Green, Ohio): 1969.

Raymond DiPalma: *Max*; Body Press (Iowa City, Iowa): 1969.

    Between The Shapes; Zeitgeist (Lansing, Mich.): 1969.

Gerald Butler: *Little Girl Lost* (a novel); Calder & Boyers, (London): 1970.

Fanny Howe: *Forty Whacks* (stories); Houghton Mifflin, (New York): 1969.

But is there really time for writing poems? And of what value is such an outdated genre, especially in view of the fact that more people seem to write than read poetry? Time is running out, and if you really have something to say, make a film or commit an atrocity: get interviewed by CBS. Unless you find writing poems fun, or hold out secret hopes that things will change. Or is it poetry that needs to change?

Bill Knott, who like many other new poets is conspicuously absent from *Quickly Aging Here* (he has a book out, and anyone who has published a book, or been included in a major anthology, was not considered for this collection) wrote a poem that tells us:

Only you can resurrect the present. People
need your voice to come among them like nakedness,
to fuse them into one marching language in which the word
    "peace" will be said for the last time.
Write slogans, write bread that pounds the table for silence,
write what I can't imagine: words to wake me and all those
who slump over like sapped tombstones when the generals
    talk.
The world is not divided into your schools of poetry.
No: there are the destroyers—the Johnsons, Kys, Rusks, Hit-
    lers, Francos—then there are those
they want to destroy—lovers, teachers, plows, potatoes:
this is the division. You
are not important. Your black mountains, solitary farms
LSD trains. Don't forget: you are important.
If you fail, there will be no-one left to say so.
If you succeed, there will also be a great silence. Your names,
    an open
secret in all hearts, no-one will say. But everywhere
they will be finishing the poems you broke away from.
        (from Part I of "To American Poets"[1])

[1] From: *The Naomi Poems Corpse And Beans*, by Bill Knott

Poetry: the attempt at peace, the momentary place where fulfillment is possible, the grand reassurance that we can indeed still change the outside world, or make it disappear. Walter Lowenfels has said it:

> If you wonder, as I do now and then, whether this is the moment to talk about poems, keep in mind that often in this age of confrontation anything else seems crazier. We are witnessing a vast outpouring of poems, each a triumph over the possibility of complete human disaster. The poem gives us that momentary dilation of vision in which we seem larger than we know; it shows us not only what living feels like, but what it could be.[2]

But in spite of the promise that poetry holds, our present situation indicates that redemption is more elusive. Everyone makes a big deal out of *liking* poetry, and once or twice a year some publishing house brings out a book called "The (insert a euphemism for "wet behind the ears" followed by a nationality or two) Poets." The implication that such a book has *the* poets of a particular category makes me suspicious, once I quell the initial dismay that I am not among the elite.

I tried out scores of names for this book, all studiously avoiding that particular limiting adjective: "Emerging Poets" was a favorite for a long time, followed in rapid succession by "Soup of the Day," "The Balance of Silence," "A Wilderness of Monkeys," "Through the Third Ear," "Generation: Some Poets of the 1970's," and finally what at last seems

---

(1940–1966); A Big Table Book, Follett Publishing Company, © 1968 by William Knott; reprinted by permission of the author.

[2] From the Preface to *Where Is Vietnam?* ed. Walter Lowenfels; Doubleday & Company, Inc., 1967—an Anchor Original.

right, the title of a Denis Johnson poem, found on page 325. Ironically, Johnson is, at twenty, the youngest poet in *Quickly Aging Here*.

But new ideas in poetry are not an exclusive province of the young, although implication often suggests that. As a matter of fact some of the "new" ideas in poetry are not so hot to start with. The "screw it all, I don't have a method for writing, I just do my thing" school had a new idea, but the inarticulate soon slump, or else inform themselves. I'm not demanding that every poet express his trade secrets or set down pretentious dicta. Yet the sullen gangs have grown tiresome, and something about the way they've accepted commercial acceptability makes me wonder. Well, new poetry can be written by anyone, regardless of age, and this book represents the work of writers ranging in age from twenty to fifty-five.

In spite of such statistical diversity, I'm sure that *Quickly Aging Here* reveals certain editorial prejudices. I'll admit to difficulty with poems that do not evoke an early, favorable response: if my initial reaction to a poem is negative, I have a rough time rereading it. Generally, I need to understand something of what's happening in the poem. This can be a story, an intellectual argument, or even a trick of syntax. But I have little success reading the grand poems of mystery that so many poets write, as if obscurity by itself were some great virtue. The value of obscurity is nothing if the poem does not offer a toe hold to the intelligence veiled by that obscurity. Without the toe hold a poem either fails to attract or seems an ugly, unbreakable nut.

On the other hand, the poem that spills all its beans early

in the game, one that hides no plot or argument (to say nothing of technique which it rarely possesses to hide or reveal) fails to draw me into a second reading. As beautiful as their sentiments might be, the Rod McKuen school of poets strike me as belonging within this wide class. Like a flower, they are easily taken apart; unlike the flower, such dissection reveals no further mystery.

No claim here that this book contains the thirty-five best unknown poets of 1970. Instead, accept it as a representation of some of the best poetry that was being written by unrecognized poets during the last half of the 'sixties. It is doubtful that any anthology, indeed any collection of anthologies, can adequately represent what is happening. At best, books are published a year or more after their contents were written; at best, the editors of anthologies make no absolutely tragic omissions. And yet, while writing this I have the lurking fear that somewhere in the group of more than 4000 poems from which I made these selections, work that might change the world was neglected. ("Might change the world!"—surely I overstate the case; or could this be a function of poetry?)

I hope this book will demonstrate that poetry of merit is being written faster than we can ever read it. Add to the writers here those new poets who never submitted work and those rejected largely because there wasn't room, and one begins to understand that anthologies of this nature reveal only a fraction of what is happening below the surface. Like a condensed book, anthologies are misleading. To rectify this, I'd suggest that readers note the magazines listed on the pages that acknowledge reprint permissions; many (but surely not all) of the best little magazines are named there; they need the support of subscribers, and their writers deserve readers.

Certainly, no library has a true collection of contemporary writing without them—for they get work into circulation much, much sooner than the book publishers do.

The persistence of poets is a phenomenon; today's poet is a small grocery store squeezed between the A&P and Acme. Rock groups learned to perform lyrics with "meaning," and have captured the attention of a generation. The graphic arts went pop and we were reminded that art can be entertaining. Poetry, alas, is not so immediately entertaining—and is miserably old-fashioned to boot. But the old grocery store is charming, if inefficient, and one has the feeling that long after A&P and Acme merge, Dirty John will still be wrapping the goods he sells individually, not in cellophane, and without Muzak.

For eventually one becomes too old to wrench his body to the sounds of Purple Fig, and the graphic arts, in spite of *Time*'s weekly Art section, are not often conveniently accessible. But before this can happen, one has to forget what he's learned about poetry in school. The child is stuffed on Wordsworth before he's half digested Mother Goose. Poetry is a chore, the burden of an educated society—something that one should somehow love. This thing to be loved has iambs, spondees, trochees—all of which can be represented with diagrams: put them in where they belong and write an essay on the second level of meaning. Where is the teacher who admits that some poets are misfits, crackpots who would be amazed if told of trochees that lurk between levels of meaning? Maybe today's exploding population of poem-writers is a reaction to the Poetry Month encountered in nearly every literature course: the teachers have failed to prove we can't do better.

But Knott has said that the squabbling must stop, that as in every human endeavor we must join together if we want to continue. The old truths only sound like idealistic crap because they've been said so often—but never tried out. It seems that now we need more than poets who just write poems. We surely need more than collections of quibbling schools of poetry: the time for that is gone.

Quickly Aging Here indicates, I think, that Knott's recommendations are already in practice. Notice the attention to contemporary events, and yet the truly individual vision that each poet brings to his concern. What is needed beyond this is a poetry that not only cries out for, but begins to show us how to find, peace and justice. Because, sadly enough, as soon as you've finished reading or writing a poem, you return to the uncorrected world that made the poem necessary. The destroyers are still in control. But the artist retains the power of infiltration, of helping the madmen to see things straight.

April 1969   GEOF HEWITT

for "lovers, teachers, plows, potatoes"

ACKNOWLEDGMENTS

My deepest thanks to the following people, whose advice and friendship counted heavily in the making of this book: A. R. Ammons, Marvin Bell, Ted Berrigan, Elliott Coleman, C. Michael Curtis, John Gill, Baxter Hathaway, George Hitchcock, John Logan, William Matthews, David Ray, and Ottone Riccio; also Mike Kinney, Paula James, Claudia Ansorge, and Pyke Johnson, Jr.; and various others who were with me during the time this book was in progress, but especially my family.

I am indebted to Denis Johnson, who gave *Quickly Aging Here* its name.

CONTENTS

QUICKLY AGING HERE

Abroad

but
if it
isn't
art
  it'll sue
    you and I
      and anyone else
          and leave a long long
            tell tale trail
                behind itself

April Lights

But nevertheless there are some other kinds of blue skies
Some other way of counting the summer clouds that stayed

There is the red moon, by October

Some other kind of February lights
Some other kind of January darkness that is deeper

A bronze rake—
A winding road to where we are this evening

Didn't You Ever Search for Another Star?

I.
did you say
August ponds
ought to have
been surrounded
by September fences?

but did you say
September fences
ought to have
been climbed over
by October peoples?

what did you say
for October padlocks
that ought never to have
been attached moreover
to November handcuffs?

II.
You'll remember us for our dark Hungarian laughter
That tickled when it laughed, that dug at the limelight

Why, I'll send you a dark silver Hungarian coin
From the mines that never saw the light of day yet

Why, I'll send you a dime's worth of Hungarian damage
That has been done to a cave that is full of Rhapsody

Why, I'll send you a silver key to the cave of despair
I'll send you a violet tonight, I'll send you a silver sword

I'll send you a silver hammer that'll hammer night and day
I'll send you a pail-ful of our kinds of blue revolutionary stars

III.
Who are you?
Weren't you their prisoner in the sedge dark?
Where has been your search for freedom?
Will you count the trees again in the dense woods
Wherever you have been tonight?
Will you look backwards where you have been?
And tell me whoever you are.
What have been your escapes?
Nevertheless freedom is as ever an intense girl angel
That speaks to one in the inane wilderness
Where has been your phantasmagoria?
Are the dark trees at war with the darklike trees?
Where has been your light
Where has been your swordy well,
Where has been your darklike table?
Didn't you ever search for another star?

4

Anything Remembered

One cloud, one day,
Came as a shadow in my life,
And then left, and came back again; and stayed

Bronze

Why, I know of a bronze lock and key
That was to be kept, and kept securely,
    And locked to the bronze sunsets

Why, I know of a bronze day in December
That I'd stayed by a bronze window shade indefinitely
    And locked the cold dream to my breast

Why, I remember a bronze thermometer at noon
That locked the sunrises and the sunsets
    At a December reading that stayed dim and cold

Why, I remember securely a bronze evening
That I'd stayed by a lamp, and kept memorabilia of the
    sunsets
      And locked the noon and the moon and the cold stars

Liquid'll

That's a pint of red daisies
That has been sent to your florist
That he has become your drunkard

White Chimes

Gin is white, for a white while,
And of its soft white dreams
One pillows oneself;
One softens of oneself,
Comfortably one mirrors of oneself;
More comfortably one's soft white dreams
Are more to do with Time, softspoken,
One loves wafting oneself away of soft chimes

Psyche

but I don't know
however it felt more like
scraping one's spareribs
for whatever is left of
the moon at the bottom of the pan

Moreso

Are you whistling
At the back of the dark hallway?
All I do know about dark life
About three rickety flights upstairs.
Are you barked at tonight
By a puppy? that would if he could
Have fed you all the dog biscuits
You wanted, or ever could have—

town

Give us time
Give us crickets
Give us a clock
could you build this wonderful town house in the grass
and put a cricket in it by this evening?

Guardian

Contrast Rooster's white feathers
With the greater surrounding darkness,
But he sings with all his blue might;
An iconoclast of old scoffs at the ghosts of the pastures,
Bespeaks of himself, stalks and struts in the eerie morning
    moonlight;
But he sings with all his white might,
Because truthfully he is our gentleman of the darkness,
And out in Bo Peeps pasture land, and morning miles away,
He is the savior, He is the guardian of the new dawn

Watts

for Sabatino (Sam) Rodia, builder of the Towers, who died in Martinez, California July 16, 1965, before the riots

1

My friend who married the girl I
introduced him to after he felt
my breasts under the steering wheel
of his parents' borrowed DeSoto,
and swims in a big jar
in the San Fernando Valley,

my friend who plucks tonsils
with manicured tweezers, and gave me
a Barlach woodcut of two agonized
women for my last birthday,
                              tells me

he's learning to shoot
with his children, teaching them how
with a gun, and last week
he hit the bull's eye at fifty feet
twenty times out of twenty.

The son who sings in the choir
wins prizes. The youngest, a girl,
plays the flute and the cello.
The middle one studies hard.

     Why?
I ask
wanting to start over.
     Why?

     We all need a gun
in the house. Learn
to use one. The first time
I fired it, they jumped.
     Now they love it. And Watts,
he says.
     Think about Watts.

2

Monday morning and the red garbage
truck shifts up the hill, jerking
like bones, like California
sliding in the sea.
                                    Bent,
with the big can strapped to his shoulder,
cigar in his teeth, tattoo on his arm,
and two flat boxes of slimy lettuce,
chicken bones, sardine cans,
used-up carbon stuck to his hands,
he climbs the path to the street
and heaves the dreck in.
                                    What
do we keep?

            Eyes, lips, heavy
drops on the neck, my friend
with his pool in his fists.

      Sensibility,
he says,
      I don't know what that means.

Scatters the water
from his wrists.

3

I went to Watts to see
the Towers. To see the sky
come at me
in thin frames, bleached
by the bluer glass.
                        The Towers.
Flying like ladders, testing
a coolness that we never
reach.
            As if I raised
myself into that breach, as if
I climbed on coiled springs

                            into air.

(Taylor over the keyboard
                        lifting
the sound so fast his hands
are spaces that the wind
pours through.)

                    Broken mirrors
and my face in parts,
the shapes of corn ears,
baskets, one thin shoe.

Thirty-three years, Rodia,
card number 6719 in the International
Hod Carriers, Building and Common
Laborers' Union, his blunt
trowel slapping the wet cement,
twisting the hoops to let
the light come in, lifting
the junk, the junk

to spires!

The way trees grow and slowly,
ring over ring.

Plates,
abalone shells, bottles,
lengths of pipe.

Against
his death.

4

Guns in warm houses.
Rifles. Knives.

　　　　Glass
in the streets and burned-out
doors.

　　　I'm saving
finger nails, cut-off hair,
nothing that sticks or stays
the same, but still
it's there. Shape of my lap
turned into something different
when I stand.

　　　　It grows.
Dead leaves and babies,
cancelled maps,
　　　　　even
my shadows, reflections in water,
loose skin over each
knuckle of my hand.

I Hear You

The promises of mother—
smiles, soft fingers
children could not touch.
You and your sisters
gliding like fish
(the tank was full
of your stare) to market
to market, sun
in your scarves, the ripple
of exquisite goiters.

You never wore a hat
except in mirrors,
your eyes were violet
under the veil,
under the knotted squares
calling me child.

But I went after you,
mother to mother,
put you together
when your bones rode you
apart. Something

was always breaking
down inside you.

Save me, you sob
in a dream, but nobody
runs like a friend
to your door. And I'm
in my own garden this time,
digging a ditch
for my heart.

        What
did you give me, mother,
that you want it back?
An empty book to put
my poems in, peeled
apples, Patsy dolls.

Each day I sucked
at your virtuous breasts
and I'm punished
anyhow.

The Hunger

And the hunger
coils out of its cave
in the center,
sprouts out of the ribs
like fireworks,
comes to that naked other
hunger to hunger,
the back of the eye alive

with two melons
under a vine.

The hunger travels
an old horizon
to a dangerous feast
not yet prepared,
to a banquet
where someone is
sweeping crumbs
from the table
too soon,
to the fruit
false as children
who never
came back,

while the melons suck
their own juices
under the rind.
The little pale kernels
shake
       in their dark
              dome.

Room

> O this is the creature that does not exist.
> —Rilke

1

The sky can't get in.
Or sun where you enter
the core of the wood.
Extravagant, burned-out
trees. There is no
provision for darkness.
Shadows flow smooth
down your skin, and the skin
of the tree thickens.
You stretch to his face,
and the flesh of your ribs
grows into his arms.
You give whatever is
possible. After so many
forests. And you are
slowly what you are
in any light.
                It happens
only when you give it
room. That milky beast.
Fed on the chance
that it might be,
it is. Destructible
as anything that lasts.

2

Lights hum at the window
like hives opened out.
They swarm through your head.
They move in the dark
of his fingers finding
your breasts.
                        And laurel.
Changed back to woman,
more lavish than she
ever was. Who is he
sliding in your arms? What
will become of you?

3

Is it because he
told you what he dreamed?
Drawing a boat through
the fountain. Carefully.
Fontainebleau's opulent
gardens. Or does it
grow to more than you
can manage as a game?
Every château in France.
Your belly is warm

and feathered. His mouth
is tasting your shoulder.
And the duck goes after
her babies in the pond.
Waking and waking and
waking, you breathe
the light from his skin.
A swimmer whose arms lift
heavy, suddenly.

4

You are behind the surface
of yourselves. His hand
strokes the outside
of your hand. Your colder
skin. Why does it
cry each time
at the tense bone until
the flesh gives in?
The sun is over
the great park. He has
gone out of you.

It Stays

What fills this house,
slides under
the weather-stripping,
wagging branches
plugged with leaves
or buckled with fruit
will never be married.

If I grow friendly,
regard it calmly
as one strokes a child's
head talking to somebody
else, it leeches
in, breeding
its own disorder.

And if I lie down
under it, make
it as real as what
I have become,
it grows around me,
shoves its way
into my arms.

Jasmine, we shake
the air and vines
catch fire.
Flesh of the inner
flower, eyes
above me coming
through leaves.

The old nibble of lies
in the dark, vines
bursting fragrant
against my hair,
hurting my face.
They climb the walls
like toads, open

their tropical mouths
crowded with roots,
saying, you've got to
feed us, cracking
the paint, the plaster,
shaking me, nothing
I'll ever tame.

Mothers, Daughters

Through every night we hate,
preparing the next day's
war. She bangs the door.
Her face laps up my own
despair, the sour, brown eyes,
the heavy hair she won't
tie back. She's cruel,
as if my private meanness
found a way to punish us.
We gnaw at each other's
skulls. Give me what's mine.
I'd haul her back, choking
myself in her, herself
in me. There is a book
called *Poisons* on her shelf.
Her room stinks with incense,
animal turds, hamsters
she strokes like silk. They
exercise on the bathroom
floor, and two drop through
the furnace vent. The whole
house smells of the accident,

the hot skins, the small
flesh rotting. Six days
we turn the gas up then
to fry the dead. I'd fry
her head if I could until
she cried love, love me!

All she won't let me do.
Her stringy figure in
the windowed room shares
its thin bones with no one.
Only her shadow on the glass
waits like an older sister.
Now she stalks, leans forward,
concentrates merely on getting
from here to there. Her feet
are bare. I hear her breathe
where I can't get in. If I
break through to her, she will
drive nails into my tongue.

The Cage

1.

It's a cage I'm building.
To put all the tigers in.

2.

A man with a cage
has tigers.

3.

They'll come out of the cage
to get me.

jensen: A Slideshow

I.

Lowercase jensen, that's dangerous.
And true: he complains, fears barbershops,
trips over women, giggles; his grin
would hang in a man's closet. But he
has his plans, no weakling's.

Born with a beard and squinty, sign
(and gun?) in hand, a Communist. Raised
to be nice, and he tried. To make humble visits.
Praised like a tame coon, petted
but he stayed whiskery inside.

jensen did everything perfect, a regular
blind kid, and was secret. Grew eyes
in secret, afraid to see. He saw
a girl, she ran away, he dropped
his cane and ran after. By now
he stumbles like anyone, and more.

jensen's habit was going home bitter
and early. He left
when they grew confusing, friends
got everything. Now he stays
smiling and late and not too drunk.

II.

He watches through crooked windows,
a kid watching. He knows
he deserves it: he saw something once,
someone he *knew*, and forgot. But looking
through crooked windows is art
in itself by now.

His car: he lives in it, knowing it's noplace
to live in, but streets are becoming, sidewalks
naked. Walking (big coat, a spy)
he talks to himself, sings, stares, stumbles;
driving he's bored, and he wants to be.
He's blue-and-white, competent, busy;
it's something to worry about, an office
to manage or family to look after, woman
he can handle.

Inspector jensen (big coat) always
at the scene; the mere presence comforts.
He tries reflections in every window, fretting.
He sees a lot, and (smilingly) is seen;
he has a theory, writes it all down
in a book. Tomorrow the case
breaks open, and he's tall.

It happened to Mr. jensen
the teacher right in class (and the woman
left him, the elegant girl
who thought he could teach her something).
He resigned from the students and the college
in secret, and stayed. Kept asking
his questions they all could answer,
singing his funny songs about being friends,
dancing his dances, dying right in class
of ignorance. Good thing nobody
said something: saved his breath.

III.

Definitively jensen: the unmistakeable
style to his defeats. He skips a little
down the wooden back steps (hands
still in his pockets, unloved almost
at dawn). He pauses a second
at the foot (to catch that precise
disappointment). He leaves the driveway
with a quick smile and something
in his step that tells you it's jensen
and he's dancing.

I'm Married

—a letter to the folks

My wife has tattoos on her neck
and queer, unmatching breasts.
She's very young, and plays
barbaric music on the radio.

She's in the john now,
washing my socks in the bathtub
and singing to herself.

When I'm late at night
she comes and sits down on my lap
and scribbles on what I'm writing.

I'm very happy.

The Story of White Man Leading Viet Cong Patrol

—AP Dispatch, Des Moines *Register*, August 4, 1968

The slain enemy resembled
an American Marine
who was 18 years old
when he disappeared.

The violent episode
was one of the strangest
in this strange war.

*

For a moment
the two young men—
the American Marine
and the white man
in the uniform of the enemy—

stared at each other.

"He had an AK 47
automatic rifle
but he just looked at me."

Gordon fired
after a moment's hesitation.

     *

Several of the Marines suspect
that the unknown white man
whom they call "the Caucasian"
could have shot first
but deliberately held fire.

At the debriefing
everyone was afraid
to say what they had seen.

Legends

1

They lived in elaborate systems
of caves, they worked all day,
they wrote long letters to friends
and married strangers.
A secret everyone knew was never
mentioned; old longings
to speak it troubled their sleep.

After long lives, they went on
writing their last wills and testaments
for years, till their last inspiration
expired.

2

They had no books to read, their lovemaking
was perfect, their wives were faithful
till they died. If they did not smile
it meant they were going to kill you.

From rock, they cut huge heads
shaped like their own, and danced
in circles around them. At the height
of their fabulous health, still dancing,
they fell off their feet like statues.

ERIC TORGERSEN

Aubade

Out into rain, out into slow streets, out into my name;
Out into my friends, my coat, my shoes;
Out into trees, mirrors jammed with my face;
Out into my life, your absence, a dangerous town.

WILLIAM HARMON

Six Sections from TREASURY HOLIDAY

xiii

Animals of the forest & plants of the field are friends to
     me & I participate in their organization
I am measured in terms of trillions of dollars
& they understand the nature of husbandry & economy
I walk among the grown-up trees with their attendant vines
& rabbits mice & terrapins are with me in my celebration
     & with me in my deep happiness

O may my heart's truth / still be sung / on this high hill
     in a fiscal year's turning.

xx

poem
is
word
list

a
list
of
words

no
more
no
less

&
vice
versa

:

na
gas
a
ki

like
that

you
do
not
need
to
know
the
key

WILLIAM HARMON

xxvii

Poor Ed Sanders: no sooner had he gotten in good with the
avant-garde by writing Poem from Jail & publishing Fuck
You: A Magazine of the Arts than the great money middle-
class machine put him on the cover of

Life

dot dot dot dot dot dot suppose we last long enough
to need footnotes explaining
meat
     explaining Mother

xxix

Now
poem & month
both almost over
& done with;

riot in Detroit kills three dozen plus
white & black, & Mr. Brown of
the non-student violent disrupting committee
says We built country & we burn it down
& Greece flat under a military dictatorship
Vietnam the same old can of C-ration worms
Red Guards katzenjammer second secretary of Indian embassy
Africa hitting the fan again
Smokey Carbuncle's visiting communist countries
&'s now in Cuba libre swapping jests with those jerks
yeh yeh
        O hot nights & sad days we count you off
& witness, witness

                    & now John
Coltrane dead

let me put that down
John Coltrane dead
man from High Point not far west of here
lived forty years of music

impossible music

                              what words what words?
      O long
songs
      Spiritual   Chasin' the Trane   Giant Steps
Cousin Mary   Countdown   Spiral
                              Syeeda's Song Flute   Naima
Mr. P. C.   India   Up 'gainst the Wall
      Impressions
After the Rain   Afro-Blue   The Promise
Alabama   Your Lady   Big Nick

            long songs
let the record play

xxxii

31 July

So let the month end: the new fiscal year
is well underway

The earth machine is falling or flying apart like usual
I plan my television afternoon

Channel 5——MOVIE——Drama
  "The Garden of Allah." (1936) A Trappist monk runs
  away to the desert where he meets a beautiful woman
  who has gone there to find peace. Marlene Dietrich,
  Charles Boyer.

tonight also on 5

  "Salty O'Rourke." (1945) A gambler who is readying
  his horse for an important race falls in love with a pretty
  teacher. Alan Ladd, Gail Russell.
until signoff with the national ditty unsingable
& shots of troops lined up with Springfields at present-arms
  & stars & stripes floating in the gale from paradise

Picture clicked off shrinks to single bright point star of
    light light years off & then vanishes altogether
into the heart of the mother
madmoder   madmoder   madmoder

meat mother muse money machine motor metal man me
    madmoder

45

xxxiv

           past all Calculation & belief it Came so huge
What colored cartoon Rodent could Nightmare or imagine It
A carrot Carrot growing wilde O Carrot wildly wildly
& bloody huge too over Polite city's placid nursing
      Landscape's blah horizon
It came from Saturn's purgatory Ring
It came from Ataulfus king of the visigoths Assassinated at
      Barcelona in 415
It came from Mercury the winter Camp of Jesus trismegistus
From Peter pumpkin eater & Unkulunkulu
It came from the Home of the free recognizing F. Franco
      on the Day of Fools in april 1939
It came from half-unlit Pee-green halls of Halitosis muscatel
      Salvation & used sheiks that made light love Safe for
      Deomoncratz & guildenstern
It came I tell you from tecumseh & Tenskwatawa
      & Tashunca-uitco
From 1813 from 1834 & 1877
& from the poet prophet Priest Nezahualcoyotl forging Pre-
      scriptions for terpin hydrate Elixir & Q-Tips & C-quens
      on red & Green gift-wrapping Paper in the lost Linen
      Closet of an Oddfellows Hall in 1520 with Luther ex-
      communicated by Leo X & Raphael & Montezuma II
      dead
It came from the Human Mind of Man & the Rosy burning
      Sled of xanadu
From Bird's milk & Celery Stalks at midnight & Hide Pock
      & Afrika korps & Eric's popskull burden

WILLIAM HARMON

It came from Hubert Hubert Hubert & the deterministic
     Urstratum of Quantum phenomena & the Belles of
     birmingham memorizing Gin
It came from those lordly king Solomon's orchids the 10
     educated toes in Stalin's burial socks
It came from 1953 & the girl Next Door
From Arnold Bax & pepsic Ulcers & the death of Scanderbeg
     the albanian Chief in 1468
It came from Berg his concerto for Violin & orchestra
& from Pavane pour une Infante défunte & the kinderToten-
     lieder
It came I say from 1935 & 1902 & 1899
From mux duRatt & young Lester leaping in & Supermarket
     Sweepings & the Edoo variation
It came from Michelangelo's statue of Malcolm x dying a
     Sunday & K K K Katy
It came from Nebuchadrezzar in Jerusalem in 588 b. C.
It came from Jacqueline's ruby queene pressed between the
     Papers of the Yellow pages in Euclid in Ohio o god
From aldershot Principia & Plutonius XC & the Trillion
     Elizabeth asylum electricities
It came from Phatic communion & ethnical culture & Kor-
     sakov's Syndrome & Anal-sadistic pseudo-Names & All
     the 1960s
From supersuds & the hysterical East following a star & bran-
     clean from Engine Love Call & the hi-freak stainless-
     Gold antennae of Troy's DonaHue hairs in 1184 B. C.
It came a long way from Saint Francis
It came Express collect Emergency from the mood music of
     Cosmo McMoon & from Tapoti—to the Melody of P'u
     Sa Man written after the 4th Encirclement in February
     1933

It came from Pink Pills for Pale People & The Blues To End
    All Blues & farcing Milky Ways & Baby ruths & from the
    Universal International harvester His Self
& from Aix-les-bains & algernon Bray & ARVN & cheeky Bob
    & Bradshaw of the Future & B. Suárez Lynch on 24 May
    1881 the most Beautiful easter in the memory of Man
From J. J. Fux & Bust her Brown & remote control Cola's
    Norbert the Wiener & the megalopolice of Babeloan
It came from Edgar à Perry & Silas Tomkyn Comberbacke
    on 2 December 1793 & Mary midnight & Mister Lun
    & zosimus zephyr & ferdinando's Foot & Ebenezer Car-
    dinal Pentweazle & Martinus Macularius & Quibus
    Flestrin & the Female student & Mark Twain
It came from bloomfountain of Vesuvius petroleum & New
    South Wails & the Briddish crown colon of Watts in
    california & The Hekiganroku
Came riding tall on the Back of a Limerick pig made of
    steel wearing this long flowing Dirty white Robe with
    Magic marker scenes of the Rape of Antarctica
It came to Me my melancholy Baby drinks too much & gruen
    Ticks
O it came from a Rose
It came from a Yes
It came from the Automon Umpyre & Sow-Jet union castro-
    nuts & Metacomet cleanser & Lifey's butter-dream of
    Detroit barbecue Ritz with the Blue Lights On
It came from the Dried-up Lips of mister Cornelius McGil-
    licuddy of the old Philadolphia athletics Baseball or-
    ganization
It tame tause see im a dood dallar in odle sings, iss & so im
    Dd too. Gd bless MD & FW & Me, ay & pdfr too. fare-
    well MD MD MD FW FW FW Me Me

Came from the Top & Vo nguyen giap & the Dalkey archive
& Engelbeng humperdumbp & simon garfunkel & Tender
Loins & the Mom of Golly
It came leaping blubber lubber from the Innard slick of
Moby Finn
From fitch shampoo & billiard Greens & Moon the mullins
Is come from the Sixtieth chapter of the Book of Isaiah
It came from Johannes de Silentio copenhagen 1843 & Maca-
pagal in Malacañang & 2-way Inventions for simulated
limousine & Yokum Von ribbentrop in F-cup Major
It came from all future Prologomena
From I say Teapot Dome wyoming & that Crowd of aristo-
crats fornicating their Monocles & orders off in the pule
at Cliveden & in the weeping stoneflint waters of the
Pedernales a River in hell
It came from Oppenheimer seeing sanskrit in the A-boom
blossom & Wild turkey drink & Quail Roost noble Prim-
rose of the Mûng Sisters
It came from Tennessee Ernie & the San Kenton choir doing
A Mighty fortress
It came one uncertain April day with Operation PLUTO
defunct in Pigs' bay & from blonded Bombshells dead
in bed of Ovadoses of Selluloid & from the Eightfold
quark
From the protocols of Dayan & wonderings of Ossian & deficit
Spending & the Lysol Gap & money glands & plus fours
& Jackson Pollock's unimaginable Genius pissing back
& Forth & round & round in Peggy's gugenheim Fire
& the Field of the Cloth of Gold
It came about Ten Thousand Years ago from the follicles of
Montgomery sutra & red squares & the Shankletown
strutters' Prince of Denmark march

From new mexico Time's picayune & the Great Speckle Odes
It came mad from Cro-magnon Adam man & Woman in cool
  Booth of Musak shopping sinner cock-tail Lounge open
  24 hours the day No cover no minimum no limit until
  the Cops came & Locke came
It came I was Alone I should have known
& it came to pass that Moroni was angry with the Government
  because of their Indifference concerning the Freedom
  of their Country about B.C. 62
It came a-frugging from the Forbidden City of honolulu Bur-
  lesque O god in heaven All Mighty that naked woman
  music & jazz-physics There
From biograph & Texas Theatre & harley & Davidson & the
  Crédit mobilier of Americard & Star & garter Chamber
  & the Gross National Manifest destiny
It came from Finnegans final Fall & all & mikrokosmos
    Hellzapoppin Götterdämmerung
It came from them
    Him me you
    O go down
    On our
    Knees
    now

Early Morning

The solitary egret
in a field of new barley.

I think of the loneliness
of angels—lacking even
the body of a shadow
to share.

Morning, in the Pastures Near Suisun

The sun gathers
last night's rain

we follow
picking mushrooms
in cowshit

Drunk Last Night with Poets, I Go to Work Anyway

The boss knows what shape I'm in. He tells me
about the twenties, when he was my age,
how he drank all night and woke up in strange rooms
with strange dolls. He tells me to get lost.

Out back is a bank of weeds I've never noticed,
and I head for them in the cold air, remembering
dogs and cats eating grass when sick.

Beneath a sky of leaves, in green air, Black Beetles
shoulder enormous stems. Quicksilver
dew quivers between leaf and stem. Through forests
of moss, I see ants tiny as salt grains
and budding red flowers smaller than these ants.
A snail dreams in the throat of an old wine bottle.
I kneel shoulder deep, careful to disturb no one.

There's a shout! Two kids struggle a tire
upslope and let go. Then lag on the wire fence,
arms hung around each other's neck, wondering
what I've found—the tire still going. Beyond,
the bruised and swollen clouds change shape
with sudden light.

For a Happy Girl

She is like a cricket:
singing all night

With her legs.

Our Garden

My love sometimes makes her shrill.
I've imagined leaving her and our sons
for the life I deserve
and should have had ten years ago
(and wasn't ready for).

Tonight the four year old jumped in the tub
clothes and all
to wrestle me,
we helped his little brother in.
We laughed and she mopped the floor.

I know they owe me nothing,
demand everything,
and trust.

And I could never understand
how a man could prune his tree
in hope of greater yield.

Death

is patiently
making my mask as I sleep.
Each morning I awake
to discover in the corners of my eyes
the small tears of his wax.

Twilight in California
for my Father

Day of hunting done,
you find this downhill climb hardest.
But where the vineyard road begins
you balk. Breathing the good scent of sweat
and gun oil, you sit cross-legged and tense,
your hunting cap brim full of grapes;
the valley cupped below, shadowless—
waiting for the wine to be poured.
First darkness sifts out of trees into your hair.

Beyond the last ridge
your Rockies pile up,
enfolding wings, antlers,
hides of slain game
that rise, now, in twilight,
with spaniels, moving down gametrails
to drink.

At day's end
your blue eyes rust
like buckshot, changing
wine into blood.

Bats

Less than Angelic
Souls who evaded life
Flying in fits
Blind to Heaven's light and Earth's
They flee to an insect portion
Twisting from their echoes

Pitchpipes of grief

The Life of the Poet

The poet is hunchbacked
by his heart
swollen with dreams
of wings, of girls whose breasts are antelope
trembling beneath the lightning
that seeds his spring: he hears the bones
of their unborn children
growing.
In this hut of his heart he lives,
and does not know if it has a door,
a mute eating crimson flowers
to make a scream, that keeps saying:
what does this do
to save my life?

His words stall for time,
slave for the mortgage on his bones:
he knows he is the fool
who cannot solve it!
yet, he goes at his heart over and over
repairing: with jellyfish, lame horses,
whistles, white cords of his body, white moths
seeking colors, odors of damp alleys,
odor of knives,

trees, stumped, putting out tiny wings
of translucent new leaves anyway.

Listening to twilight schools of spooky minnows
tuning their scales, he has got the drift
of this sea he lives in;
in nights's sea of star-
fish that stops all eyes
he sees the boats go on,
overhead, with cargoes of ocarinas
and red melons—

Swimming to any shore, he finds himself
there, already, with his black horse
and his cart, heaped with salt,
paying back the sea.

Not Writing

Just finger prints and drool
where I dozed off on my paper
to someplace in my head
where she is nameless
        forever, where

I am blind and speechless
traveling to her from steam
            through glazes
that rise from her mind

There are speeches of light
in aquatic temples
diamond blades of black velvet fangs
reflections on gold givers—

I wake to dreams I can't control

Refrain

We are two people
Sharing the same bed;
       — I remember the twin beds
        and the diverse timetables.
When your teeth grind,
I would share your shaggy nightmare.
I move closer to you.
We are two people
Ticking at the supper table;
       — the sudden evening pushed us
        into awkward chairs.
The knives scrape the ceramic plates.
I would caress your acid breast.
I nudge your foot.
We are two people.

At Ten o'Clock in the Morning

Walked around in a daze all morning
Taught my first class without talk
Just can't seem to get us together
Like poems that I wanted to write
Cold coffee made me dizzy &
Puke in the stuttering lunchroom

    Cold in my nerval coat
    of acoustic ceiling
    tile walls
    linoleum floor
    formica table
    chrome & plastic chairs
    I could not move or hope

Couldn't say much to my colleagues today
So I smoked while my stomach jellied
and sweat in the student men's room
like fetishes smudged on the metal walls
Like curled hair caught by fingerprints
on the tissue dispenser, I locked the vented doors.

The trip for hell and self

> —Matter is veiled life, Life is veiled mind

Must have begun through Friday
noon I ran
to greet you Spring was freaking

me out. The asphalt walks, soft grass
and silver
Paris necklace. Again you dressed in purple.

Mexican wrought hand
silver, your
eyes are blue, that a fine man

gave you. I'll drive your
old sedan
on a quest for gypsies

to read the smooth wet palms
to give up
our habits of eyes meeting

The whole thing's a ritual isn't it?
the red lead city
like a fungus before me

Seeing such things
through blistered row windows
white panes, wrinkled pink walls

Eyes that possess me
hand of understanding
emptiness that brings no shame

Wife, widow, teeny bopper
Restrained sighs
claw tracks in my shoulders

Oh°!! Mother!, is that what I'm doing
is it my fault
that I don't grow sleepy

you are grand and I'm not afraid
to say it
sugar comes in all forms

they are your red silk pants
for heavens sake your scent
I'm no fool to smell it

Smells like parsley, pepperoni
I feel you
move beneath me fine stroke hands

you must be mountain air
in this poem
I kiss your breasts

your nipple rises firmly while
I suck it
and press your plastic buttocks

So we can not even be friends I wish
to kill you
What does it mean to say we are lovers
and how can I make this message felt

these things are dreams
that steam away with light
and I am water left for sipping.

On Blindness

Smell the rug. Smell the wire that holds the chair together.
Taste my writing.
Smell the flesh on which I work my magic spell.

It is impossible to write; too many themes and senses
Super heroes
Ego hangups and needs to walk about mumbling Kill, Kill.

We are all going to kill someone. Killing is the
way of life.
Notice the line form of this poem. Should one kill one's self?

It is too easy to kill one's self. No, that is not it.
It is much too hard.
Live hard; sit on top of the world; go down like a legend.

Waste time, Oh waste time. There was a time
when I could watch
the tide go, could watch the tide go by.

Feel the rug. Feel the wire that holds the chair together.
Hear me write.
Feel the flesh on which I work this magic spell.

To Rimbaud in Hell

I. (the encounter)

When last I walked there,
not quite unlike you my brother,
it was indeed as you have said,
and at times quite different.

Spider webs glistened in the mornings,
after rains, after miraculous nights
and the one with large eyes,
    —I am sure you knew her,
still runs in the evening in flowing sheer gowns.

You are mentioned at times,
now here, now there,
perhaps too often, too easily I fear,
but alone now, finally, it bothers me
    little.

I had hoped of late
to follow you to Africa,
but as you see me here speaking,
there is no more need for those
    drunken crusades.

Hopeless thousands left just yesterday,
I've news today our leaders' graves are
    robbed,
and countless fools on ramparts
shout their notions.

Aye, yes, she has cast
that same jeweled dagger to my chest,
but were I once more young
I would have her again.

II. (the talk of the two friends)

The wolves howling overhead at night
make sorrowful noise in the fields,
books are read and reread,
and wind whistles through cracked windows.

Whole nations squabble in patriotic grandeurs
and on their limits, as on the lace trimmed hem,
and in their depth, as in contact,
    —the love of that final moment,
we have both dwelt, a while.

Soon castles are built and are rubbled,
sand drifts where blue flowers grew,
and walks by the sea are found useless,

for the hunger, and ritual are gone.

The church has grown thin,
Seldom leaves its perch by night,
makes long flights in quest of fat,
and rattles its bones at sounds in the attic.

There is little, save rotten meat,
powdered rock and the rust of iron facades,
with which to fill out stomachs,
empty as the place wherein we stand.

III. (the separation)

In this dark place, as in past bone caverns,
random draughts pull and point apart,
In this humble way I raise my hand in gesture
to salute this meeting and await its passing return.
Many await you,
I have naught else to say
while they sit in sleep, grit their teeth,
and wring their haunted hands.

from THE MARLBOROUGH POEMS

Rose do you know
the Marlborough
Do you know The Marlborough
Rose

Rose
I see myself in rooms
with creatures who think
they are strange

One room shows
a fur coat, gloves
& boots of spotted tiger
a sword, candles & cutting table

Please take care
of those ancestors
who glow with sorrow
One room is hung with my bones

Old ladies walk close halls
that leak rain the wind blows
Rose do you know
My rooms in The Marlborough

Rose ghosts who
float in loose robes
inhabit The Marlborough
Rose

2. (Roof of the Marlborough)

At the end of an evening
discussing the bardos
with a traveling friend
it occurred that
the roof of my building
was not far above.

Legs like rubberbands
we shook with speed
climbing stairs nearby
unknown, used by few people
to catch dawn flashing;

Green about the old machinery
Violet pulsing through the maze below
we felt clear light of morning
raise our hair.

Waiting for Lunch

He's been sick
and waits for lunch sitting in bed
    What'll it be today
    Tuna fish, yesterday's lamb
    Vegetable soup, something weird?
He takes coke. His finger probes
a bloated belly yellow below
    The navel. He has nothing
    To say. Friends of the family come
    With eyes poking about the sickroom.
They're looking for germs.
Mrs. Gnarler drew some up
    Her twitching nose.
    His nakedness shakes the
    Friends and the family.
The pale mark sheets have been exposed
and late at night they've heard him laughing.

Zombie

He's off somewhere
is what
his old friends say

When their eyes can't
meet his
while they're talking

Associates & strangers
say he's
bold though somewhat ashen.

He is confused
and talks
to them like a bathroom

Mirror. He does not
know where
they are caught.

Stars. His eyes grow
brighter
& see through them

Finger of Necessity
Postal Area #29, Los Angeles

Twice recently young girls have
            given me the finger. The
    first was on the freeway, she

sitting close to her boyfriend turned
            with sure purpose and aimed
    at prominence, seatbelted in

two lanes over. The chemical shock to
            my system made me feel so
    like they wanted I chased them

for miles trying to think of something
            to yell back. The second a few
    minutes ago standing beside a

drugstore would have been easy to
            go back by but I just waved
    like oh another one. It must

be something in the atmosphere, Scorpio
          on the ascendant, or maybe they
          were bored with the just looking

and better this than what I didn't give,
          much better. With one buzzoff
          finger she became the mother

of my invention with her red
          shirt and her hiphuggers
          and her flowered vinyl belt:

Hey cat lady, you eat it.

The Oracle

> *Do not ask of me*
> *I am the hooded one*
We are here to consult the entrails
for your departure.
About my cave are several signs of life
on the verge of their future
which may be read collectively or not
according to your mood.
Notice that I have no scroll or prepared text
as we approach the first enigma.

This squashed pigeon says one thing,

> *You are still young*

And this black mule, still bubbling,
> *Do not submit yourself*
> *to your own mind*

Upon the cistern ledge this fish
inside a fish inside a fish records that

> *Life is passed*
> *in the simplest of circles*
> *not in the expanding universe*
> *where everyone's mythologies overlap*

And the wormy goat stomach,
what do you think it means. Look closer.
What do you think?
It is a simple admission that

> *All advice is vague*
> *and plagiarized*

Ah, look, they fly, they fly away,
my beautiful birds, my gulls . . .
an omen of another sort which means,

> *A number of changes will come*
> *and leave you depressed*

The fire there which, as you see, is going out
will go out, and this garbage will begin to rot
tomorrow, which all means something else again,

> *We shall be left with fragments*
> *of an order that is not our own*

And as you pack these secrets up
and leave me here among my vitals
with a lot of emptied animals,
I must insist that you mean well.

From: BODY POEMS

Stomach

lunch paper sinking
into

the lake surface
the lake bottom

sleeping frogs
snapping turtles

Elbow

cradling my funnybone
like a child
I didn't mean to hit:

the dull ache, the surprise
at kissing myself
there

Heart

an earthen
sound:

60 seconds later
the two all-clear
whistle notes

Brain

a flashlight
looking through the empty
limbs

Appendix

one boxing glove
laced up
and ready

Navel

hold the phone
down here   see
if she can still
hear me gurgling:

my Long Distance
mother

Ear Lobe

Suck Creek, Lover's Leap

(we all know
what happens there)

Forehead

the two main lines
of your palm fit
exactly over the ones
at the top of the
bridge of your nose:

what have you forgotten

Skull

a folk remedy
for the lovesick:

share a meal
of turtle meat

then tack the shell up
for a birdhouse

Scar

the one chance
I will ever have
to go to Finland

is a long lake
frozen to my leg

Inner Ear

the girl on the dime

gets off one night
and meets me there

Bags Under the Eyes

the turnaround place
at the end of a lovers' lane:

why is that car coming back

The Truckdriver

a man surprising himself
with care for somebody
who is
out of sight if there at all

what is it
(some mother's charm
against the highway)
makes him take time

> *in this dark*
> *the sun is four broken lines*
> *on the pavement*
> *like electric fencing*

> *tuck in your feet*
> *there's nothing showing*
> *of two children*
> *in a big cardboard box*
> *standing in the righthand lane*
> *of NC 64 going north*
> *outside of Hendersonville*

> *when a carwind goes by*
> *hold it down from inside*

this is our house
to be safe in
and afraid together

before the truckdriver
will skid to the near shoulder
slam his door and uncover us
like a news item

he will be a father

closed up in a cab
full of too much light
who thinks in the second
instant of seeing it ahead:

my anger   my horsepower
would barrel through
dogs & cows   piles of brush
& rows of boxes
anytime but now

on this morning:

a searching sound like a crownfire
of love and sheer luck (wind and dry branch)
runs with my ignition

Nickajack Cave

Your recollection burns in my lantern,
shadows me down this ancient tufted ear.
My eyes relax in darkness for your sight.

My hands touch stone that wears water
and I am almost out of sight now almost
gone, but listen for me. I mean to be lost

for years surviving to come out somewhere
telling a tomfool story to filling stations
and chenille shops who will have heard it

before: beneath this place your version,
you long drink of water, is yodeling
like a bloodstream, garbled sleeping sound.

**

You are here beside me wondering
if I know where I'm going. You are
there inside singing to a swarming

room. You are the survivor who
found another way out. The cave
itself is nothing but your skull.

You take me past the ribs and kelson

of a pleasure boat through the broken
teeth of an admission stile to where

the audiences don't remember you
with bear hugs for a stranger—to
blank holes filled with history:

the Nickajack tribe and the Union troops
and myself fallen shattered from the ceiling.
You stand with me like sleeping rubble

dreaming of form and you nap in these
cubbyholes hanging upside down
folded in a brotherhood of yourself.

***

This cave confuses us. Meld of rock
and dung and water. Our voices blend
in a noise that tumbles the lock

of the hill and lets us out—in a
chord that starts the sacred harp again
humming in the earth like a dynamo:

What wondrous love is this
O my soul   O my soul

Feather River Valley, 1956

moving with her
above the stream sound
held by the 4 x 4 stilts
underneath the dance floor
at the back of the restaurant bar
stuck out over the water
I was learning
I am learning

what she has to do with laughing

(that old sound
forming under the floor)

on the kitchen stool
my wife is
another culvertful
of laughing waters
(Minnehaha)
the same substance
the same rushing away

of a dark watery time:

so in the slippery bank sound
all the people-ducks begin

Choosing

for Kittsu

Floating with your head back
up to the ears in a river
you can hear a lot of lives
you didn't expect: an outboard motor
starting up beyond your sight
somebody's sinker taps against a drum
two kids are yelling mouthfuls

In the general flow
are sounds you might make yourself
and ones you can only imagine:
garfish moving along the bottom
water moccasins curling into tree roots
Chickamauga Dam upstream
imperceptibly giving way

Half in air   half in water
your eyes awake   your ears adream
with soundings   the mind can bob
and understand where it is

Alone on the shining surface
buoyed up with creatures
in such a dangerous sleep
I have created children taking chances
underwater   at night
edging with their fingers along the bluff
above the river   jumping barefooted
into a cellar full of broken glass

And one recurring child too young to know
what's risky on a ledge
curious only   about me   down here
too far away to reach him where he turns
like a dummy falling   lands flat on his back
each night   on the mattress pile of my choice

Safer in my dreams than in his
and falling   more certain of love
then the tiny fishlike fact he was
when both of us forgot he might exist
a strange bit of marine life   sticking
there on its own   bringing up questions
of freewill and time and the possibilities
that we broke
against the motel mirror
in plain water glasses thrown to curse
and celebrate   our combining image

Wide awake   you chose   I chose   crash
following crash   not him not then   but
to lie there accepting   floating as we used to
in riverwater filled with silt   and muskrats
and sunken boats   and boys swimming

For nothing comes of choosing really
in this bed we have fallen into

Lay back your head and listen
to whatever will be with us
to the waters pressing on each eardrum
for the life inside

Paces

Invisible hammers
make a soft anvil of my throat

touch tastes like shade

I scoop well water
    the taste of the tin cup
    on my tongue
    by this mountain

I will not return
to the city
the house door
swings
in the quiet moonlight
    on the window
    there are shadows of pine

Again Beginning

late
a storm of birds

wind under the branches

a scythe
lying in the fields

a road   cold
wind
cutting my eyes

yellow horizon line
and crystals forming

waking inside
the locks of hurt
held in the throat
the chink of stone
in so many of the words

Messages

Weeds in summer
a wolf call over the branches

rain
and the pouring of loneliness
into silver threads

the tree's dark bark
and yellow in the wind
a call in the meadow
for mating

the quick silver charge at dawn
mist rises from water
around bark
from my mouth

tell the dawn
wings fly
battles cease

the skin
of this morning water's
still clearness
is enough

Soft Rain

The lines beyond
the mist
are pale enough

We hold
something like a heartbeat
there is this flutter
in our hands
that understands water

The Eye

Silence

we are given
ladders

find no end
to walls

then a long time—

Diamonds are cut
in the eye
of the absurd

a deer moves under snow leaves

SOPHIA CASTRO-LEON

A Letter

The wind
skims down the path

I have decided to live
at the edge of an old wood

Beyond the compression
of the smallest stone
an angel bleeds

It is winter

The white memories
of your caresses
clip the edge of nerves

The fire colors
stay lit in the bones

If you come this spring
bring the morning wood
rolled in your breath

Come by the bend around the fences
where there's sunlight
in the pockets formed by the trees

Under the tongue of wind
that comes wet
from the ocean

Turning

Don't leave
wait
until the hawk
gets off my head

there is the light of a flood lamp
and black walls

a late voice
consents

Bright masses of flowers
erasing the mind

in the larynx
a wolf gate closes

Noon
light
slips over the mountain stone

past shade
the sound of water

fools
make cages

DENNIS TRUDELL

The Art of Poetry

You can say anything.
That a young marine charging up a sand incline at Saipan
suddenly thought of mittens on a string.
That after hours in the museum
all is quiet; the Rubens in Trafalgar Square,
for example, stay well within their frames.
That the lake of the mind no longer at civil war
must be lovely and quiet, with delightful small fish
nibbling near the surface.
That Rasputin's toenails
must have been clipped by someone:
where are such traces now?
That the impossible sea
is heaving tonight at the flanks
of a ship with lights and music . . .
of many ships, carrying an unguessable number
of indiscretions, and not a few smokers
considering the jump.
That a flagpole doesn't care —
how silly to march past it on a fine Tuesday
in a small group dressed the same
and hitting the left feet at approximately the same instant.
That the air above your sleeping son's head
is as holy as rain.

That nothing is perfect: an unpleasant woman
said on television tonight I should think of my stink.
That the next person you turn to
may be the only one you'll ever have a chance
to love more than yourself.
That a statue is not a fiesta.
That the snow makes so little noise.
That a car goes by. Slows down, stops, backs up.
Pauses, the motor whirring—and drives off.
It is midnight and October in America.
The small towns are left to the leaves.

The Guest

If one day you are walking along
and suddenly decide to ring the bell
of a lower left flat near the center
of the city, and you do, and a woman
in a paisley housedress answers, asks
what you want and you can't think of
anything to say, just stand there
until finally she smiles, says you
must be Margie's friend and Margie
ain't home yet from whatchacallit,
beauty school, come inside and wait,
and you walk into a coffiny parlor,
nod at a chairbound old crone who
smells like wet carpets, sit paging
Life for May 7, 1963 and listening
to the paisley woman wonder from
the kitchen whether you've ate yet
and enjoy sauerkraut—and as you
say no you haven't and yes you do,
although you hate it, the door opens
and a girl in white with improbably-
colored hair, gum, and a rather nice
figure comes in, says hi and you say
hi and start to introduce yourself
when you hear the housedress coming,
ask instead to use the bathroom,
and follow the shrug and forefinger
into the dining room (nodding at

the paisley on the way), then duck
into the kitchen, out the back door,
and into the crowded kitchen across
the hall—whose door happens to be
open and where some sort of family
reunion or something is going on
and a female NCO-type is urging
everyone to come in and be seated,
and so you follow into the adjoining
room, are seated, and start helping
yourself from various bowls handed
round, meanwhile making small talk
with those on each side, a fat man
with a cold and a woman who suspects
her son has not married wisely,
and joining in the general laughter
at the jokes of a horny-looking man
spilling food at the far end—which
proves a mistake because as your
head is back in mirth, a hard roll
smotes you on the shoulder and you
can't decide whether it was thrown
by the small boy behind the peas
or the thirtyish woman with slattern
eyes who keeps looking over at you,
and who either by design or accident
slips into the chair on your right
when dessert is over and everybody
is herded into an ashtrayed parlor
to watch slides of the host's recent
trip to Columbus, Ohio: which slides

go on and on until you begin losing
interest and stick your hand up into
the beam of light and start making
shadow animal heads while everyone
either laughs or whispers "Ssshh"
and the host says "Okay, let's knock
it off," but you don't and he says
it a couple of more times and you
hear even the horny-looking fellow
and the small boy and the woman
with slattern eyes join in with
"Hey, enough is enough" and so on,
but you keep doing it until the host
moves cursing to a wall and turns
on the overhead light just as you
softly click the front door shut
and hurry across the hallway
to knock upon its twin.

Gambol

November—but the town
is warm and shines. Sunday
morning, Pennsylvania. The
fronts of these white houses.

Follow the cracked sidewalk
to the river, where dead leaves
have been moving downstream
all night, are still
moving . . .

But the light makes where
they're headed bounce like
coins. Think of balloons. Fresh
air moves through my heart,

Juices the old wanting
to be in Paris—or maybe,
since the TV show I watched
while burping my month-old son
had leprechauns, in Dublin . . .

My wife, one month a mother,
watched us from the sofa.
She's back there rocking him.
I go for the Sunday paper.

To be in Paris . . . but the sun
on a bit of Pennsylvania weed
is also nice. Think of porches.
Sing ah well—nobody has it
all; this is most of it.

Going to Pittsburgh

In and between the cities
the go-go girls are bluffing.
They really will not step down
and lie on a corner table.

The men prefer the ones
who look most like coeds.
The men have come there
from factories or softball.

Their eyes do not love
one another's eyes; their
wives or girlfriends are home

changing sheets or channels.

Their in-laws fail to
understand them, their sons
wear faggoty hair — Something
is hungry; it is not fed.

In and between the cities
the night is ungenerous.
The pizza and hamburgers
are thin; hitchhikers freeze.

The car-hops don't jounce.
The motels are unfriendly,
their flies bite. Their walls
are sick of self-abortions.

Something is hungry; it is
not fed — In the soft suburbs
the martinis aren't working.
The heads of industry are sad.

Their candidates don't win.
Their alma maters won't let
them re-enroll; their suicide
notes have comma splices.

In and between the cities
the stares of the blacks
are causing cigarette burns
in beds of the middle class.

The husbands do not know
how to load the small arms
they have bought for summer.
They think often of Sweden.

They think that in rooms
behind drapes in Negro bars
the Navajos learn karate.
They fear for their stereos.

Something in and between
the cities is hungry; it is
not fed. This is no season
to learn the names of birds—

It is no time for that.

The Jump Shooter

The way the ball
hung there
against the blue or purple

one night last week
across town
at the playground where

I had gone to spare
my wife
from the mood I'd swallowed

and saw in the dusk
a stranger
shooting baskets a few

years older maybe
thirty-five
and overweight a little

beer belly saw him
shooting there
and joined him didn't

ask or anything simply
went over
picked off a rebound

and hooked it back up
while he
smiled I nodded and for

ten minutes or so we
took turns
taking shots and the thing

is neither of us said
a word
and this fellow who's

too heavy now and slow
to play
for any team still had

the old touch seldom
ever missed
kept moving further out

and finally his t-shirt
a gray
and fuzzy blur I stood

under the rim could
almost hear
a high school cheer

begin and fill a gym
while wooden
bleachers rocked he made

three in a row from
twenty feet
moved back two steps

faked out a patch
of darkness
arched another one and

the way the ball
hung there
against the blue or purple

then suddenly filled
the net
made me wave goodbye

breathe deeply and begin
to whistle
as I walked back home.

The Poet Tries to Turn in His Jock

> The way I see it, is that when
> I step out on that court and feel
> inside that I can't make the plays,
> it'll be time to call it quits.
> —Elgin Baylor

Going up for the jump shot,
Giving the kid the head-fakes and all
'Til he's jocked right out the door of the gym
And I'm free at the top with the ball and my touch,
Lofting the arc off my fingertips,
I feel my left calf turn to stone
And my ankle warp inward to form when I land
A neat right angle with my leg,
And I'm on the floor,
A pile of sweat and sick muscles,
Saying,
Hilton,
You're 29, getting fat,
Can't drive to your right anymore,
You can think of better things to do
On Saturday afternoons than be a chump
For a bunch of sophomore third-stringers;
Join the Y, steam and martinis and muscletone.
But, shit,
The shot goes in.

In Praise of BIC Pens

Others always skip over the word
That will bring the belligerents of the world
To the negotiating table, if only

I can get it written, or will
Teach thin kids in Woetown, West Virginia,
To rebound tough and read Ted Roethke—

I'm writing along in a conspiracy
Of birds and sun and pom-pom girls
Lines to cheer old ladies with shopping bags

Waiting by their busstops at 5PM
Or lines to get the 12-year-olds off cigarettes
Or save the suicides in gay-bar mensrooms

Or save the fat man from his refrigerator
Or the brilliant boy from color TV
Or the RA private from re-upping for six

Or the whole Midwest from wanting to conquer Asia and
the Moon
Or the current president from his place in history—
Oh, if only I can get it written

No one will burn kittens or slap little boys or make little girls
    cry
Or cower at cancer or coronaries or plain palsied old age
Or get goofy from radiation in his cornflake milk—

If only I can get it written. But always
When I get close to the word and the crowd begins to roar
The common pen skips, leaves the page blank—

But you, BIC pen, at nineteen cents, could trace truce terms
    on tank treads,
Could ratify in the most flourishing script
The amnesty of love for our most dreaded enemies:

The ugly, the poor, the stupid, the sexually screwed-up—
Etching their releases across the slippery communiqués of
    generals and governors,
For Behold you can write upon butter, Yea inscribe even
    through slime!

But at nineteen cents no one pays attention
To the deadwood you shatter or the manifestoes you slice in
    the ice—
For who would believe Truth at *that* price.

Getting Short

His day closes like a dry mouth.
Next day the ropes are frayed
as usual but the sundial proves his innocence.
Generals play jumprope in the riverbed.
The garbageman approaches with the leash.
They will release him when it rains.

Section the grapefruit into shrapnel,
gaze upon it. Time is anything longer than short.
They have draped skin over the targets.
He is forced to shower while the armada sinks.

Imagine eavesdropping
on the birthpangs of one's own first breath.
His eyes wait like shrivelled propellers.
And he hears them, tunnelling.
The green horse will wait in the park for a century.

Just for him she's growing a mustache of bullets.
"Do not anticipate . . ."

But he longs for this homecoming—
his pajama bottoms folded like eagle wings,
the evenings heavy with apples and full canteens,
the memorial pillars crumbling under the pressure of the dead.

Every morning the girl
brings him the news: schoolbuses not
plunging into gorges,
a man who has lived his whole life
and is still alive.

DAVID HILTON

The Newlyweds' Accident

In the accident
some shoes without toes

farther on stretchsocks
and toes and

beneath the major portion of his torso
a suitcase full of stew

his wife.   Crowds
of cameras

disperse with mementos
and ladies aids hastily

collaborate on a donut drive
as sirens consume

man and wife
beyond the diagram of grief

now dissolved to *fin*
and the orphanage's outing

at the cinema
is done.

And now bedraggled angels
tumble out of trees

this sight to see and
gawking skywriters go

crashing into schoolyards without bailing out
as two bodies

form finally
through the mercy of motors

a genuine
union.   Oh! on this green earth of love

accidents everywhere even
on TV midnite-movie doctors

ecstatic to doom us alive to
oxygen tents and go

and confer
but these fused two

escaped for their drive.

Childhood Ambition

He is a timid man
And for free
Will allow you to look
Into his baldspot.

But he will say
"Trees"
Timidly
And pat his puppy's head
To pulp before
The thing can bark.

"Trees" he'll insist
His dome growing gnarled.
And the delicate designations that gleam there
Will collapse like a column
Of solemn commitments.

"Cigarette" he'll purr
"Time for some smoke"
And he'll whistle a tune about hair.
The lights of great cities will dim and flicker.

Then you may cross.
Hatchets
Will appear in both hands.
Eunuch-like
The forest will slaver to serve you.

You will rock on the spines of your enemies
Peaceful
As a puppy

And you will not want
To leave
Alive.

DAVID HILTON

Zoo, with Lamp and Chairs

The last of them escapes
to the joy that scratches at windows.
In a bottom drawer
other weapons . . . wings and scales sinking
through the ancient reservoirs of smoke.

And language exits, a warm trickle
as when someone whispers *Pain* in a deaf child's playroom.
The black
panther's sobbing
leaks down again
from the ceiling crack . . . and the steady
"Boom-k'boom" of amorous camels.

The paper child is playing with candles.

Inside the darkened fistula
it is story-time—a promise
of windows tightening
with cold:

When the moths return with mouthfuls
of the sun, the sky will reveal
its animals.

Sunday Again

We stopped by the seashore
to read Roethke, running
to the water through
our cigarette ad.

For Love's sake I find you
a pretty shell,
and we walk barefoot as birds
while I do my reading to the three grimy gulls
attacking the last of your potato salad.

Look at me, it's our Sunday again,
and his words
are only his head
whitening now
in his dark time, a bowl for deep roots.

But God Bless the Bone!

Ah, fond widgeon—
once, done with reading,
I drove you moaning
near the pain of bone.
And ever since I sleep
married to those moans,

as the same waves fall,
the same birds scatter
with trophies of trash
and the same rocks shatter
ten-thousand miles of water
and the familiar decay is born on the beach,

while I slap sand from your feet,
gently, reading . . .

And always down the beach, just below the cliffs,
where the huge arch breaks from the rock-line,
that small movement seems now
the beating of birds driven low to the sand,
now a whole family of dead
children running
to greet us.

Hang On

When the sun whitens
Breathing is just another transparency
And ducks
Find their lake
Thickening

Too late too north
This November
Turning black
As you please at 6 o'clock.
Think filthy thoughts instead: think
Of Jesus
Masturbating in the desert.

On the way home each night
You see the ducks
Plunge slowly, they shake
With lethargy. But save it,

Hang on. Listen
At 6
You clothe yourself in muscles
And exhale prayers.

I Will Give You a Purpose

I will give you a purpose.
Carry it with you
like an umbrella.
It will protect you.
The rain spits on all of us.

Marina

A beerbottle armada bobs in the rainbow
oil slicks by the calm mouth of the marina.
Cabin cruisers bumping against the wharf,
so many dead whales to be raped now roped
to the whaleship's side so they don't sink.

Drink in hand, laughing, her sprayed
beehive hairdo jerking spasmodically
as though prodded with sticks,
my mother's head appears and vanishes in
the round porthole of my vision.
I crouch on the dock holding a halo
to her face, seeing if it fits.
She disappears for the third time, and
my legs are stiff from the awkward position.

I walk to the end of the wharf where
a cruiser chugs out of the harbor's shelter,
wallows in the trough of the first waves
like a drunk stumbling into the storm.

Waking Up in the Woods

Jesus! she's thin. She squirms in her sleep
like a white worm crawled halfway
out of the sleeping bag.
I light a cigarette, moving away
under the trees to watch
the cyanide dawn creep through the leaves.
At my feet a praying mantis weeps
as it devours a honey bee,
tearing apart each armor band
of its golden abdomen.

A *Single Candle as the Presence of God*

—for Rona

We are the one for which all light
is shed, we are the coming together,
the estranged and divided returned to their source;
we are the single moment for which the candle
sheds its blood in silent ecstasy.

Things You Left Behind

I

Your white raincoat hangs
against my wall like a barnacle.
I tried prying it off with a crowbar;
No use.
I tore up half the wall
around it, but
its hard white roots had
already grown into the masonry.
I gave up.
I began watering it instead.
One morning there were two
tiny mushrooms on the collar,
though they were gone the next day.

II

A broken string of beads
behind the dresser.
You put them there,
commandos on a mission,
where they might roll out
at night and stepping
on them I would
crack my skull on the
carefully placed end table.
It is some consolation
to know you were thinking of me.

III

There is, if I cared to sort it,
something of yours in the garbage.
For instance, that grapefruit rind:
You carved it with your own hands,
hollowed it out,
squeezed it
for the last of the juice.

Dead Wasp

Your abdomen still twitches, probing the air.
She says if you fly into the house I must kill you,
which makes sense. But when I have
swatted you, she screams and takes your reflex
throbbing for suffering. What can I do?
There is no way to act rightly.

Being and Wind

Another day when being
alive is its own reward;
The wind defines me:
        hair in my face
    the open places

        between buttons.
I am its absence
stepping through space.

The Visitor

First he rushed over to a
large chair
lifted its tail and
kissed the ass of the
cat, sleeping

Then we had lunch
You eat like a pig
my daughter said
I love v-ape juice
he replied

Then they played house
But I want it. No
it's mine. She
cried. He kicked the
cardboard walls down

What shall we play now
I won't play with you
You break my toys
Why did you invite me then
You're a coo-coo head

Lovers
Of
Blue
Elide
Loves
Instant
Annulment

Wind, Intrudes, Lifting Day,
Cantabile, cantabile,

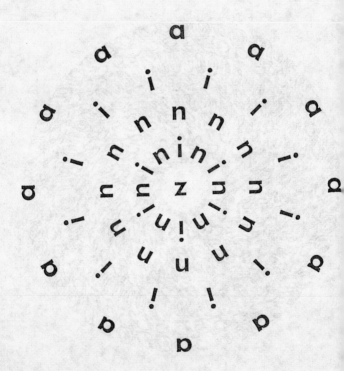

Conspiracy in Iowa

There are some very ghastly faces
pressed against my windows
these nights and something
big has been in the potatoes.

Have you ever been to Lone Tree?
Where a bloody man sells
geese and leaves their heads
by his pump til they're skulls?

There is a man in Iowa who keeps
Pancho Villa's skull in a leather
trunk with mementos from Japan,

a small portrait of his mother.

Out here where a dog's tongue sticks
to his own frozen water, catfish
winter sullenly under the ice,
moving their tails in long, slow thrashes.

Where faces watch my wife undress
and there is nothing in my mailbox
but letters with windows, or a ladybug,
or an ad for Farm/Sport Thermal Sox.

And if you've ever been to Tipton
you know they don't have parking meters,
but four saloons, a courthouse, three
variety stores, a hippie and a movie theatre.

And I tell you there's trouble
right here in Iowa City when a boy
would stand the cold, far from
parental love, T.V., to see us enjoy

one legal pleasure in this wretched land.

Rod Slemmons' Dream

Here is a place you've never been,
where a sea wind shifts the dunes
eternally, rocks refuse to weather.
These halls can be narrow but a turn
will bring you to a ballroom
or a cocktail party with old friends.
Sometimes you walk on scarred
linoleum, fishnets fall out of a warped
closet but dust won't ever rise here.
There are one hundred boarded rooms
and one where sunlight falls,

but doesn't fall.
You think: "This must have been a pantry
and over there they kept the ice."
but then you see your sisters,
still little girls playing parchesi
on the window seat.
You're twisting a knob to a door
you have to open. Something
painfully boring is chasing you,
but the damn thing is stuck at the top.
Losing interest you start juicing
lemons, pressing down and twisting.
Why are you squeezing lemons?
There is no water, no sugar, or a glass.
A naked girl sucks your earlobe
and you get an erection.
You touch her softly, with love
and she becomes a little girl, twisting
indifferently away from you.
So you go to the sail-loft where
it is as silent as the world of the deaf
and the air is always fresh but still.
Two men are stitching a sail
and you know you shouldn't
but the polished oak and colored numbers
are irresistible so you step into the room.

Attic

Failing in business, grandfather
did not go West or drink, for
the depression was an act of God.
His wife, children, Herbert Hoover
were forgiven, victims of his mercy.
Twenty more years he sat in this
uncomfortable chair charming old
ladies in Kalamazoo with his
gallantry and Latin phrases.

Here we are when mother was pretty,
grinning some great family joke.
A minister from Peoria, college
professors, shrews and midwives
clustered in fumbling intimacy.
The uncle who was electrocuted one
Christmas by his treelights steadies
my sister on a nameless dog.
Vulnerable and out of focus

we patiently smile, forever.

I hear faintly the excitement
of my children misbehaving below.
The old men buried grandfather
in Benton Harbor but here he is
among confirmation papers, diaries,
invoices and unfinished things.
Crouching to the pane I watch
my daughter waddle through my
garden covered with petals and green.

When Beulah Did the Hula in Missoula

Snow in August, and people
talking about it all the way
up to the cheap hotel which
wasn't cheap and smelled like
popcorn, gas leaked somewhere.

Nothing moves that mountain
but weather and earthworms.
Signs say pack a shovel, pail,
axe, beware of grizzly bears.
It's a long way from Raspail.

A bad place to camp, much less
mate, where game are counted,
tagged, and Indians stay drunk.
At Chenonceaux the river doesn't

run but history is *son et lumière.*

When fires come they grab men
off the streets, mills close,
Smokey waves from the bank.
An Indian tosses coals to forest
muttering burn, you mother, burn.

Where Racine is not Wisconsin
there are cuckolds and baroque
ladies leaning on their pillars.
Now, held behind the gills,
my bug-eyed trout mouths,
help, I'm starving, oh God.

A Hermit Advises a Monk When Things Are Bleak Indeed

Soon the wind will be gentle
in the morning, but I don't know
if you will still be alive to
celebrate Spring like last year
with Spaghetti and wine.

Let's click heels and doff hats
one last time to the good ladies;
drink beer and pick off ticks
while the canyon breeze is warm
and our talk is to each other.

The five-stone drug has dried
your skin; you're half here
and the rest is hunting them.
Somebody is lost under the stars
and the green chain takes a break.

All those berries are poisonous,
that bright pool is alkaline.
Come back you fraction-man,
the Indians are drunk. That bear

they're skinning looks like a man.

Here's my shanty with old tires
out front to sit on, meat-loaf
in the oven, a mountain to stare at.
A man could drink with his pigs
or have a quiet joint if he wished.

How clean the wind is tonight.
It comes off the western coast
and after all this way the sea
is in the mountains bringing memories.
Will you enjoy some wine and music now?

The Crazy Lady

The Dirty Man makes an obscene invitation
to the Crazy Lady in the Italian courtyard
of the BPL. Korea she yells, Korea.
That's all you think of. Korea she whispers.
She is very crazy, the crazy lady.

Drunks moan in their sleep when the sun
slips them into the shade. The splashing
fountain makes them wet their pants.
Such a peaceful place to sit in the summer,
clean gravel paths and little orange trees.

The Crazy Lady confers with her lawyers.
She bawls them all out, dismisses a few,
then she pleads, weeps and they come back.
She is suing all of us: me, the drunks,

the library guard, the Cuban who fixes

the fountain, even the children and birds.
The Dirty Man pulls at his jug and leers.
He moves with the sun closer to her
dark corner. He shows us what he wants.
His fly is open; he is very dirty, the Dirty Man.

Oh, but there is no cause for alarm.
Every day this happens, see, they are lovers.
They hold hands and talk quietly so as
not to disturb. Soon they will go
to the Commons, by the wading pool,

feed squirrels, talk of what they'll
do when she gets all that money.

Card Burning in Central Park

I open my family magazine, pretty
girls, whiskey bottles and then you.
I show my wife. She says you're a troll,
your teeth look crooked and why do I
run around with fuck-ups like you anyway?
Some questions don't expect answers.

Mountains and bad weather have done
something for me, I feel my Wheaties.
They're crunchy and the morning paper
clues me in on Ed Slocum's lost cows.
Last night a canyon wind blew over
gas war signs, drove magpies into town.

I know you're unfit for service,
even the cops won't beat you publicly,
but old-timers can pick out desperadoes.
Out there in the sheep meadow with
Mad Dog Anderson, your eyes like Saturday
night you cup the flame to a cheroot.

Trumansburg Fair

In her little tent Honey Bumps
lumbered out of sequin finery,
cymbals banging each victory.
We stood, tanned and drunk
in the dark pit, feeling handsome.
A loudspeaker announced cattle.

That lady's rubber dummy had
a wink, a leer, a cocked hat
and a name I've since forgotten.
That man boards my bus at
night, thumbs my magazine,
is only cigar smoke at dawn.

We fingered our girls in the
House of Fun, weird laughter
and blackness made us private.
The firemen's beer made us dizzy
in the sun while farmers with
beasts trampled chaos everywhere.

Our world swung wide
on the corners as we slept;
only stars hung over
the lake and pastureland.
We woke heavy-headed before
the city, holding our rumpled girls.

The Campaign: Letters from the Front

A FOREWORD

Just short of the isthmus, the court
phrenologist, puzzling the import
of the seven lost adjectives
in the Book of Skulls,
brought the columns up short
signaled the lighting of torches,
high noon though it was,
and retired to his cart
not to be seen again for several weeks.

FIRST LETTER

        it is a strange land, sister
and while the knitted banner, tribute
to your craft, hangs from my cuff bringing
no small measure of reassurance
I am less and less your brother for every hair
that's added to my beard
        though votives to the optic nerve
and visual purple have been prescribed
astigmatism runs its course through our camp. Mother
it will not be long now

151

                    my arms have grown wrinkled
and my forehead—well, expect the worst
                    and sister, wed Stefan
if you must, though I fear his days of sight
are numbered, lensmaker or no.
                                        It is a strange land
to be sure, and the yellow eye hangs always
just below the next rise. We measure the distance
to the straits by the grain's height and
if we do not sight water by harvest, this campaign
like all the others shall end I fear

in white-blindness and brain-frost. Father
rest his eyes, would remember well

SECOND LETTER

                    Muriel, wife
I have coupled with the enemy and my parts
are no more. Pray that what is in your womb
is male, for Nortus
fretting also as his curls go limp
has called upon his first born
                    these ditches and pits, wife
how may I explain them
                    painlessly shallow
the mud on their sides like mucus.

152

                                        So many
have fallen, turned on their backs like turtles.
First the erection, then death
                and Muriel, at last
my brother's anklet has been found, a spike
driven through it, fixed to a wooden curb
hardly noticed for the yellow moss upon it
                I cannot bring myself to dream
and must devote the Moment of Cycles to fantasy
and the small seasons to your memory
                and did the flesh on the neck
of Jan's commander part and run, driving
the counsel from his tents?
Did his commander eat his own droppings
and demand that the games of his childhood
be played at sunrise? I have lost my footprints

in this fearful country
home of my brother's bones

THIRD LETTER

        Uncle William, your nightmares
stir me. The graph, the arch and the fifth corner
are only blotted pages in my ledger. Here
the leaves die on the trees
        the red chevron on my sleeve
has brought some measure of respect, little
though that matters to me, and
as Foreman of the Grove, I am served last
and most generously
        we know nothing of the winter here
and all pipes are laid aside at the mention
of brown in its less subtle shades.
                       Uncle
I am nourished only by your gothic spices and
the wagon, when full, lacks anything, I say
your herbs, Uncle, and the glow
of pipes around a dead cook fire
and the night shot full of holes
and the day running on
        You, Godfather
do you keep your cave tidy and free of smoke?

I spit on you! We have secured your island for you
        the sky is pulled tight and knotted
the ocean stagnant, the fog weaving in
        then the clouds that roll in my ears
and the smoke that chuckles and scratches
through my brain, cramping my eyelids
        William, can you see to my affairs.
Peter, your questions escape me.

Carlo, you came out here half dead
and I am only doing you a favor

FOURTH LETTER

        I am addressing your ribs now, Adele
as I see no other way to keep you whole.
I resist complaint, for the boats heave off
only when a perfect silence is achieved. And
only prow-foam will flesh you out again.
SEND PICTURES OF THE CHILDREN. Are there five
now or seven as before
        orphans have stolen my mattress
but I can hardly begrudge them this small comfort.
Marguerite, your husband's orderly
informs me of the youngest's illness.
SEND PICTURES OF THE CHILDREN.

Does Karl still sleep through dinner and appear beforehand
with his trousers unlaced. Such a clever child
           Adele, I lost your good-humor
on the quartermaster's barge, and it is ribs now
every night. Does this flatter you?
Are the children aware of Uncle Niles?
They must be old enough to understand
           no word from our son at the front.
SEND PICTURES OF THE CHILDREN. The lower keys
have disappeared and the leather ones are hardly adequate
           no words can express it. I must risk
an indelicacy. Your breasts, Marguerite
shall be clamped about my nights and your groin
shall be the smallest unit in the distribution of glass.
Have I made myself clear?
SEND PICTURES OF THE CHILDREN
           our orders say only to be on board
according to rank and sorrow.
This is the big one. Operation Spendthrift.

Another beach and another form letter
announcing our son's misuse

FIFTH LETTER

        Son, do not waste your fifty coins through
indecision. Your mother joins me in beseeching you
(Testing—Testing) do not lift a skirt without good reason
and let not the reason be one you hold in your hand
        very soon I shall give birth.
At an inappropriate moment. In battle perhaps, my ear
to the sight, my buttocks filling the plastic saddle.
The adjutant went into labor this morning
attended only by the kitchen help who welcomed
the break in routine
        (Testing—Testing) Wallace
your constant attentions annoy me. These trees
should be free of obstacles and this role you play
unauthorized next of kin
is a perfect approximation of a grossly subtle rhythm
        but dearest son
visibility is not merely a matter of simple cleanliness.
All senses shall be employed.

If only they were pot roasts (Testing—Testing)
or static, in layers, near an unavailable horizon
            these instruments lack sophistication.
Childbirth should not be undertaken by amateurs. Wallace
you must force my hand. This child needs a father and
all in all *und so weiter* though I do not think this dust
could have driven us to it. Son, son, son, (Testing—
Testing) Son I cannot explain
            how messy we all become with our equipment.
Nothing is unreasonable if you eat it.
It's all a matter of fashion anyway.

If we finally meet them next fall, I shall
definitely consider raising my hemline

SIXTH LETTER

            Sister Vivian, after a year
all we can remember is that we came by water.
My mattress has tides. Too many shapes come
then go under the influence of an unnatural moon
            Walter brings ointments
but his nails are dirty. Clara lives for fresh linen.
Natalie, sleeping in flurries, dreaming pink
lives for a needle. I do what I can
            Monsignor, I regret to say that
your subsidies are useless. Nothing is certain
till we weigh it with our hands. I remember how
my habit billowed on the bell rope. I never guessed

I'd find myself trapped inside a nightgown
with a lizard up my veins
        Mother, there are things
I should have told you when you were younger.
About the darkness in the sleeves of an amputee
the fox-fire around a hemorrhage
sewing up a sack of flesh
        Sister Ursula, a prayer is a gunshot
and though I enjoy them after a fashion, the boys sing
in their own contractions and pay me with beef
        Mother Superior, the lawyer
you will marry gave me a child, and the child
gave me a basket of pain.
            In such a country
the clouds fall of their own weight and the wind
sits like dirty water in a sink. Still

though our bowels are numb and trembling
we wait for moonrise and a rush of surf

POSTSCRIPT

        Brother, this fist
this unnatural flower blooming in my sleeve
        Mother, this razor of nausea
this tightrope cancer and treaty of germs

We've fallen in love with a fractured bone.

        Father, this convocation
of wounds, this recruitment of calluses and claws
        Sister, this final frame
this metal lover with a beam in her eye

We've fallen in love with a hole in the ground.

The Front shuffles into our kitchen.
We set the table with nightmares.
This is the meal we've been waiting for.

160

The Busted Lute: a Baedeker

These droll slices of spring like a novel similar
To our first impressions off the boat: Antwerp, city
          of diminishment
A challenge to our finding Library or lodging—
          this diminishment,
This pale attic inverted in a degenerate season, a sea
Of illogical Europeans & the echoes of old friends' comments
          on the weather.
Small talk like a tumbler. Brief visitations from a
          soothing grief . . . !
Why *do* I come back, when the mirror tells me more
          than age,
When my hope is more than axiomatic, a reflection
          lacking balance.
I giggle to myself—a way to forget
Those cities in the hands of troublesome women,
          Antwerp, a pleasurable
Similarity in her women to my lost sister
          part Flemish herself.
We pose as burghers finding the feel of it not unfamiliar:
I know my mysterious home is old as well;
I no longer fear its riddle, my calm is jelly-like, inert.

The Andalusian Lute: Another Baedeker

In Granada baths are *de rigeur*; therefore the freighters
Present their weary passengers with a bar of soap upon
Discharge of certain fluids. The florists are ill-mannered
Flicking their wrists at more than mosca-flies, as
     my editor warned.
How *did* I land this assignment? "One lip kisses the other"
Conchita was fond of saying as she thumbed thru my notes
     unnerving my
Extremities. But this is an unfair comparison.
     Granada fingers
My memory of that sour-dugged priestess of swing but I must
Dance! Lord knows, all else is fabulation
(with a bow to my mentor) at least here I am or
     here I am . . .
Granada is famous for its epistemologists. If nothing else
And that latter is all that's here with a technique all its own.
This is why the articles requested are not forthcoming.
     Dear sir,
The fluid stains; Conchita's long dead; and I'm up for
     that bath.

162

Haiku

The pine trees explode
the birds at dawn and cradle
their exclamations

Our house stores sunlight
in baskets and sets it out
for the evening fire

The small drunk turtle
challenges the morning wind
to race to the pond

Some Few, Some Very Few

some few, some very few, possess death
when it comes and hold onto it—
a daguerreotype displayed
next to their bed it becomes
a conversation piece referred to
as calmly as an ivory cameo bought
somewhere in switzerland.

                         this old woman—
the link for me to quantrill's raiders and
strawberries stolen the summer of 1889 and
hunger kept
on dusty shelves—

this old woman
took death into her body years ago
with quiet hospitality she understood
its need and could not refuse
though this new expense would
exhaust her small resources.

she was once a large woman
a matriarch whose authority grew complete
as she buried two sisters four brothers
mother father six of her children

husband. turned to the business
of her own funeral she has made
one last count of her household goods:
examined the souls of each
of her survivors: inventoried
her life's decisions: now she waits

while sewing a dress
from the remnant memories
of ninety years she says death
is cold to her: she does not like it

evening news: st. louis

willard wirtz, secretary of labor,
supports humphrey the news says
over in central illinois
the big muddy was reported
to crest safely under flood level
because of recent heavy rains
snow flurries with slight precipitation
were predicted for st. louis
johnson received an ovation
in st. patrick's cathedral
a late bulletin announced
that martin l. king was shot
to death tonight on a balcony
in memphis
there were 3,238 vietcong
killed last month by allied forces
mrs. mabel burnham won $630
in the kxok easter egg contest
the pope still declines to make a statement
on birth control
                                        4 april 1968

upon which to rejoice

A slight stirring darkness
ordered us to hesitate.
Somehow we had found it.
The hard earth was matted with brittle hay;
the soaked-in acid smell of animals
stifled us in the first instants;
rough branches of juniper
scratched against the mud walls.
The night was cadenced
with the warm, heavy breathing
of a woman who has born a son
and, resting from her labor,

looks upon her child.

We had not surprised them
or disturbed their night.
Unmistakably
they had expected us and we,
in turn, had sensed they would be there.

No one spoke,
which made the stillness reverence;
while provision for her comfort
became our awkward male concern:
adding to the fire, another cloak,
tethering animals. He took
our embarrassment with gentle
eyes and helped us do again
what he had done before we came.

But we had nothing else to give
and our silence was inadequate,
though none of us knew why.

The Home

I

They walk dangerously
close tonight . . .
Those mad little girls
I can hear their voices going
The cat, sunk in his basket
           never reeked
with quite such sour fury

And the program—
       that wall-eyed twig
of a momma
Miss Klister
dead on arrival
from Munich
What possible life
did she think she could glean
from
      a Peter-Pan Bra
Clairol
      and the dry-heaves
      at midnight
We were her specialty
delusions of poesy
      and the like
a delicacy among the street inclined

and the asylum babies.

And how fine it was
to be not quite
             really crazy
among all those
stately and profound insanities,
To be taken so seriously.

Can you remember
Claudia, edging into oblivion
                  sideways
       with bulging eyes
Watching it
       just below her right shoulder
slip up like the tide—
       talking all the way down.

Was it she
to whom
you gave Vaseline
with instructions
for Yusef
"that Arab"
She sat shiva
later
set fire to her room
mourning Claudia
who had somehow
got unstuck

And Karen
big bosomed and foul
puffed-up like an adder
threatening imminent explosion.
With two bright
                    discs of ire
she would hold you
secreting fluids all
the while
suffusing the room
                    with a heavy
                    aromatic damp
Red curls boiling
over a brow
            flawless
lucent
those perfect features
            untouched
I remember the bite
            of her nails
her thumb particularly
along the cheek
            up to the eyes.

II

In that room we shared
you slept
          badly
your bed
          in tight formation
          right angled to the wall
you took things as you found them
Mine—
          askew but slightly

That room;
oceanic,
we dove and surfaced,
as was officially encouraged—
the great mirror
a vague and
occasional shore.

All about
into the night
the ceaseless cry and cackle
of the sea-fowl
hunting
          there was never quiet
in our wallowing
          world

Who gave them first—
the land flowers
               ferns and dogwood
establishing a precedent
               we looked at each other
               with startled eyes
and could not name it.

Say it now then
now that the danger is over
Speak of the resin and the burning pine
the rich and heady smoke
rising
         to shivering lips

We bore our love
like some strange
         transplanted organ
shameful,
         necessary—
Gills
to survive
immersion
in that deep
         wet world.

Chameleon

What of this loving
that we do   is it to or with
                    one another
Here
in this narrow
        soft hollow.

We are both
            swamp creatures
cold-blooded
and green
        in the grass
and thicket.
            Grey under
            the pond stones
We blend
        succumb
                and are reconciled.

Unfurling
      Our pronged tongues.
Saluting the fly
      before encompassing him.
      Flight is nothing to us
      nor   the seasons.

We shall lie still
together
in the mud
our twin pulses
beating
till the bright hawk
           dives.

Snips and Snails

I

This scored tissue
of rain
divides my sight;
reserving half my vision for itself,
withholding it
                    from the far side
                              of the street.

Once one
had plaited
a flowing sheet
of clear plastic
into a short rope,
and fixed it
by a thick
              brutal knot
to the parched railing
                              of the fire escape
And there it hangs   three, five years since
                              trailing rain
from its soiled lacy
                    ends.

And another said
                "Clitorises
        are getting
                longer,
                you know"

It was his choice
        to have her
        pass nightly
                        below his window
                        naked,
                        her pink clit
        swinging freely
                        like the clapper
                        of a great bell.
And he would fall
to her
        as loosely
          as an unbuttoned shirt—
        and enter
                and curl within,
        tighter than a pearl:
Where do we
get the bits and pieces
to fill our secret bag?

Chewing gum
               tobacco
        clots of dust
and a soft pear
lint
      and ink
  stained tissues
              spewed out about her
              as Miranda
              fell backwards
              in the
                   lurching
                 subway car.

Out of control
we seek only to be diminished—
Thinking to
lose our hapless strength
through the stratagem of despair,

As if that would close
the unsleeping eye.

II

Charles Lloyd,
you are among the heroes
              of this season
              of fevers,
and Keith Jarrett as well—

You pluck the cherry
You mouth the cherry,
You spit the cherry forth:

> pit and skin
> and
> tasty meat,

the highest
>   ripest fruit.

You know
>   that shame and terror
>   lie with pleasure
>   in a pocket between the belly and the spine
And yet
>   that from that place alone
>   the fire-flowers grow:
>   Threading needle like
>   filaments of blue
into the rank tangle
of the larger roots;

> bearing down,
> suckling
> our tenderness.

I am so near
I can hear the petals
tremble—

> splayed on the forest floor;
> two   unmatched
>   scintillating
>   lips of light.

American Poetry

—with apologies to Saleh and Simpson—

Can it roast a duck?
Can it have a baby?
Can it do an adagio dance?

And will it dance
With grease on its mouth?
And blood on the darkest part
Of its inner thighs?

Miller

And that was the hottest summer
I ever knew in the village;
All day, drinking my
Sweaty beer, wearing my
Literary undershirt, the one
With the holes in it,
Writing the novel to end all
Novels . . .

With your hat and shoes and
Bag, with your fingernails
And tease-me mouth, wearing
No underwear, you came
Every night without being called,
Without knocking,
To proofread the new pages,

To check me for errors.

This is a message from California,
Where the traffic grows more absurd,
Where I am failing in my
Belief in accidents.
This is addressed to all the hollows
Your body no longer has.

And what it says is that
We all must eat something—
It is the giant's decree.
I am therefore sitting down
To dinner,
Which will be a glass of blue, cold
Water
And your sweet , blind eyes.

Who Is the Ratman?

—After a seventeenth-century Dutch etching—

To dream of rats in childhood,
Nibbling your eyes like frosty
Blue grapes;

To dream of the white wine
Those grapes could make;

To become a wine drinker,
Going home, following
The line between the
Cobblestones . . .

My dirty hands rub my eyes,
My head hurts:
No one to make it better.

Who is the ratman?
Who is the rat man?
Call the rat catcher
With his dog and smoke
And trained rats.
When he is done,
Share wine with him.

STUART PETERFREUND

Percussion, Salt and Honey

I

I sit drinking wine,
Talking to a traveller
With no memories.

Down in the street
Is a man falling down.
I have been watching him
All afternoon.

Sometimes Nancy shakes me
Into the morning. I am a
Traveller with no memories
About shaking to sleep.

Or do I go smoothly
With my wine, striped sails
On the red sea?

II

One winter, in a
Survival suit, I went
To sleep in the snow
In the meadowland above
Taughannock.

And as the stars gave way,
I woke up,
Thinking I felt the
Ground move. But when I got
Up from the drift blown
Around me, there was one smooth
Impression of my body.

The snow I melted
For a morning meal tasted
Sweet, the taste of blood
Or of another mouth.

III

And that summer,
When I saw myself in my
Sweat one day, unloading
Crates in Chicago;

And that summer,
Lying in the furnace with you
To remind me of the ashes,
I think I learned the talent:

The sound of a beehive on the ocean,
The sound of a spice drum.

THOMAS HANNA

I Make Fallout Too

Today the wind is from the south:
a thousand magi enter the Saarland
as if to blast open the apse of the northern sky.
They are senators-designate,
my missionaries,
sent to lead the Celts and Goths
into some hot weather ideas about flesh.

You, Maria, are repentant: all your slits
ache
from being open so long,—your eyes,
your various inventive mouths
have tasted enough reality:

The countries of the east
are tired of the shifting crust of earth
under their feet, the perilous politics
of our west.

Maria, we will pet and fuck the day away,
until,
tossed in the air by some black beast,
we must await Omar Khayyám,
the high priest,
my tax examiner,
who will break our fall with his
long arm of words.

The Leader

—For David Ray

That the green angel of nature
might weep at his feet,
he would twist and torture
the air into mushrooms and
then be seen in heaven.

And he will not stand it to be
otherwise. And it galls him
that for killing
he must trust to others:
the stars are too small for his anger.
He would catch us each
by his own finger,
wherever we are,
in huts or pockets of green.

Vietnam Turnpike

The disastrous condition:
the organdy road,
Sparkle Plenty in conference
with Senator Morse,
me riding
down the New York Thruway
wife and child bunked
in the back seat
in the new wealth
of my Dodge Dart.
A vortex crawling up
from the side of the road,
the unseen hitchhiker:
a friend: a fish-tail
setting up, lifting up
the rear end of the car,
moving it back and forth,
casually.
A condition, an organdy road,
a certain confident step. . . .
Sparkle Plenty comes,
silver-maned, witch-jawed
to witness the wreck.
Sen. Morse calls attention
to it, Jeane Dixon tells me
about it before it happens.

My child, wife, dolls floating
inside the cabin,
National Safety Council cameras
hold the thing
in slow motion for my eyes.
They float past me,
Raggedy Ann- and Raggedy Andy-like,
and the windshield floats in many pieces
admitting them to a different inside.
I, clumsy, slow motioned,
play footsy with the pedals,
an organist in church.
I make a certain step.

The road is silver-maned,
slack-jawed,
I debate.
I debate the view of Helen:
this face could not launch a thousand ships.
I debate Troilus and Cressida.
I debate Paladin.
I debate my
brother in law the State Department.
I take blows on the head from police:
I hide my earring while they beat and beat me:
I am not Van Gogh.
I will not give them my ear
even if I do love them.

I can clear all this up
with a phone call.
I call the permanent observer

from South Vietnam.
They tell me just who
Pham Khac Rau really is.
There is some mistake.
He is a private citizen.
He used to be the PR man
for the Saigon Government.
"Friend" I call—
"Do not leave me in the street!
"I, too, am a private citizen!
"I swear we are alone!
"Let me in!
"Don't leave me bleeding in the street!
"My car broke down, believe me!
"Open up!
"I'll tell you about it,
"about Raggedy Ann,
"Raggedy Andy!"

The Downtown Swan Thing

My women surround me,
Isis the Swan, Lila Hopeful,
the ancient streets contain them.
The bricks,—big spenders—
shower us with awful gifts
as we walk look at geese/
watch the paratroopers fall/
like meteorites.
I drink them all in—
bricks, girls, invaders—
start thinking about Esta,
my only Jew,
going nuts over Johnny Cash.
I agree with her.
I agree with everybody!
The kids I taught in college
enlist,
my own bloodcells
become the ultimate deterrent.
I lean over Manhattan
to take a look at the Narrows.
The heaven tilts,
and ashes to ashes
we all fall down
victims
to galloping horsemen/words
trapped in the craw.

Christmas, Ibiza, 1966

> —For Ruth

I had asked you to try again
to turn on the light,
to try your luck on that faulty switch,
but you said it wasn't worth it:
if it was going on, it would have by now.
No, I said, it's just the switch,
it has to work one time in 100 anyway—
don't you believe in anything?
        You laughed and I said
I will show you the power of belief and in one shot
verily the light was on. It was because you
had just said that when a child closes his eyes,
all the world goes black,

and that you made me remind you of it.

The Song of Casyor Brioschi

Stand there hours, Casyor Brioschi.
Have fun standing feeling bitter,
reminding people of a stunted lamp-post.
Your looks aren't hot enough to light those windows
across the street. They know no pleasure.
They are strict mothers, guarding little Honey.

Don't try to say you love poor Honey.
No one will listen to a stunted lamp-post.
You are disgusting, Casyor Brioschi,
and you are wasting everybody's time. The day is bitter
cold. Pigeons huddle by chimneys and windows.
Honey's mother sits inside: "It was a pleasure,
Sir," she glared at you. Her eyes rattled like windows.
To see you fumble your goodbyes to Honey!
The slobbering exit of Casyor Brioschi.
You found out that too much love is bitter,
like too much wine. Stand up, Lamp Post.

Be proud. Never be a slouching lamp-post.
Remember, you are a Brioschi!
You are of a race of great and bitter
men. Move your hot feet across the tar with pleasure.
Ring the doorbell till it oozes honey.
Make the shades wink in the very windows.

Ring your heels in halls until the walls are windows,
until the women whisper "he's a man, is young Brioschi."
Be tall and strong. No one thinks a lamp-post
will fall down. Give your second smile to Honey.
Save the first for her mother's pleasure.
Tell her, "Mama, Mama, don't be bitter.
See now? Your son is docile. Don't be bitter.
Open up. Open your heart like windows.
Please now, give your urchin one small pleasure.
His gut is cold. It rattles for tea and honey.
Bang on it. It's hollow as a lamp-post.
I am your little boy, Casyor Brioschi."

That's the way of the bitter tribe Brioschi:
leave the lamp-post, crash in through the windows:
The proverb says that bitter honey gives more pleasure.

"Boarding of Pan American Flight 207 Will Be Delayed Ten Minutes."

These are an airport's bones: the pairs of lovers
opening and closing their embraces
like shellfish breathing, and the knots of children,
anxieties and parents at the parting
of now from ever. We consult our watches.
There are people weeping under the Pan Am sign

and at the insurance kiosk. Shall we sign
for flight insurance, we who are clock-bound lovers
of life, this life, still ticking in our watches
and in our ribs, and through our hard embraces?
Or would we crash in vain? This little parting
pinches us with omens and the children

have radar in their minds. We are all children
leaning toward the tower for a sign,
a wink, a warning. Are the clouds parting?
Is the sea? Will lightning part the lovers
and solder strangers into weird embraces?
Each eyes another. Each stranger watches

through shadowed eyes, his shadow. A skyhop watches
baggage carts. A mother counts her children.
Nuns watch each other, but a priest embraces
the host of us and grandly makes the sign
of Christendom, to wave before the lovers.
"And where is the such sweet sorrow in this parting?"

a co-ed quibbles as the time of parting
is endlessly postponed and we rewind our watches.
". . . *will be delayed ten minutes*." Yet the lovers,
self-winding in their passions, are like children
who will not mind the clock or any sign
except the metric of their own embraces.

". . . *will be delayed ten minutes*." These embraces
define our limbo at the edge of parting
ten minutes deathward. Under the Pan Am sign
we wave good-bye for anyone who watches
and then become each other: parents, children,
enemies and comrades in the arms of lovers.

We peep between embraces. Through midnight watches,
our dry lips parting, we prepare the children
for a sign of consummation in these lovers.

The Gentleman's Garden

The gentleman's garden
is held secure
    by a green electric hedge.
Not even a cat
can cheat the hedge
    whose eye admits no evil.

The gentleman's children
are dumpling good
    and will not touch the hedge.
Among their mother's
roses they play.
    They pluck their mother's roses.

Their father whispers
against their cheeks
    Good-bye. His beard is bread.
His children play.
The woman they hear
    beyond the green hedge, screaming

My hair is on fire,
my face is on fire,
    is nothing, is no one they know.
Their father is gentle.
He would not murder
    something they could not eat.

The Husband

He'd never wrung the
neck of a rabbit, a
goose or a sparrow, not
any until
in the night
with a cat
at the back of the cellar
he strangled and strangled.

But why? said his wife
with the chill on her nipples
and fur in her mouth
and the cat eyes staring.
Why did you bring it
why bring it to me?

And the thousands of cats
were the jaws of her question, they
mewed up the night from their
thousands of fences.

He sucked at his tongue and was drunk on the juices.

Wedlock

He does remember.   Back to the bloom
of everything, his own undoing, how
on the honeymoon his earlobes grew
to bladders full of music she
insisted listening.
The wet white melon always on his plate
and the waiters waiting.
How licking secrets from her sugared lips
she bathed him nightly in her breath
and bluebirds in the tiger's mouth were singing.

Beyond the tropics.   How a hand could shut
their wooden room, could lock its corners,
how the cans of fish they ate of
swam in rainbow.
And bowls of blood the soup she served
in which her eyes were floating, he
remembers and her eyes' reproach
as manly taking up his spoon
he ate it all,
he sucked her down.

April Thirty-First

And call it the maiden ladies day.
With lavender water, with attar of roses
flutter them out of their Back Bay houses,
out of their West End pots of flowers,
out of their North End east wind closets;
ruffle them out of their cotes as pigeons
flush and feather, the maiden ladies,
under the sun their silken dresses
kiss kiss kiss in a ringworm pattern.

And summon the beautiful blue police
with blown-up butterfly nets to gather
all the drunks in the Boston Common:
swoop and capture, swoop and capture
Billy-the-Bum, Sweet William fallen;
raise them, shave them, all in satin
dress them just for the day and dance them
down down down to the Public Gardens
arm in arm with the maiden ladies.

BARBARA L. GREENBERG

In and out in the Public Gardens
swan by swimming by duck by tree
by bridge and river and flowered path
they'll dance, the maidens, the maiden ladies
sweet and sweaty, the red-nosed rummies
ringing their buttocks above their thighs
like wedding bells. Come down to see.
Come down to see and pack a lunch.
And nobody laugh.   And *nobody* laugh.

The Victim

A thin wool coat was the jew of him.
Young, he saw it hanging in the attic;
left it hanging, sleeping in the attic;
never let it kiss his back.
Grown, he pawned it,
kept the ticket,
went on eating buttered steak.

At that long table where the guests are faceless
he was faceless, chewing on his years,
exhausting through the ciphers of his nostrils
anonymous smoke, like locks of loose gray hair;
and couldn't cry, with nothing to put the tears in
and nothing tragic moving in his veins.
Reflecting on a teaspoon he discovered
his teeth were dead jews' bones.

An awkwardness on Sunday was the jew of him.
A special sense of meat and milk, an eye for noses,
an appetite for fat, a matchstick cross
to crucify a puppet—rot and nonsense.
The jew of him was limp, his life was limp,
a this, a that, a chronic indigestion.
Oh God, a pill, a tonic.

In his blood
the desecrated temples burned.

Rain falls on synagogues in Amsterdam.
In Prague. In Athens. In Jerusalem.
Rain falls on synagogues and stains them gray.
Rain in Venice
invokes the odor of canals
where Shylock flesh decays, decays.
He smells it, he
refuses to be disgusted, he
despairs of knowing
what hideous things his own breath might be saying.

A lump of soap is the jew of him.
A yellow band, a hill of bones, a pound of glue.
The thin wool coat a scarecrow wears
warms no one.
He wags on a leash of wind, a tail of wind,
a jew, a jape, a nothing much, an echo.
Jesus, he cries, and *Hitler Hitler Hitler*
but not a sparrow answers with his name.

Poem for a Dead Aunt

I dream you naked on a float, blown up
enormous and attached to strings
like, in a bright parade, a rubber clown
whose painted membrane might,
at any moment in the hot fat sun, explode.
All that trapped air. As if your heart
in a last fit of love let go
a jet of gases and ballooned your skin
ten times beyond its former sense and shape.
Tipped to the sky, your nose, your nipples,
capping the hollow breasts like lewd berets,
and the appalling contour of your belly
that the wind wrinkles . . .

Skipping beside you like a faithful poppet
I blow my message in a paper horn.
"All a mistake," I cry, but nobody listens.
"Terrible error," I tell them. "Cover your eyes
or cover the body over." Nobody does.
Confetti sprays upon us from dirigibles,
from lungs of fever, and a band brays.
"Cancer," I bellow. "Cancer and the plague!"
and turn against you with a sharp thing in my hand.

Never to Visit You

Never to visit you
morning held the circle.
My eyes marry
hour by hour
white stripes cut
with your invective.
As one always ruined
you may be consoled.

Curious, nobody turned
to discover the air
moving always.

A direction turns each of us—
I would give the words
differently.
A dry month. Lives.
Sheep hold the wind.
Night after night
privacy changes.

In the News

In the news
still.
The earth beats
the skull.
Secretly the nerves
blush less vividly
than before.
Meat hungers
in meditation.
To have seven tulips—
hardly
too soon.

Pale New Lights Cling

Pale new lights cling
to flourish your pillow
differently.
Silken emotions carry
you carefully.
Taste and touch
started these fields.
Your riches sleep
out of speech
passion all the while
behind.
Pale, having loved, the master
enters your window.
All the privacy to be
trembles.
Somebody's home
at the center of this show.

Her Skin Runs—White Stripes

Her skin runs—white stripes.
The season suspended forms
to count.

His own mounded darkness stains
mirrors.

The maze, all of privacy
to be, trembles.
The candles, like western stars,
grotesquely answer
teeth. Within, sensual inlays
acutely run.

Secretive, the nerves dance.
The loom of days washes away hooded night
always.

The Inhuman Rain Rejoiced

Black, the sun floats melting,
Solitary rocks, moss glow,
Naked, something cringes.

The sun carries mounded darkness
On the side of inland mountains.
Nobody will believe the baby.

Disguised, unnatural ways grew.
High the dark ocean meditates
Something ailing, nameless—a cask.

The elementary mists clutch
Needles fleeing black pastures.
Nothing walks moving out from thorns.

The Magic Idle Windy Spaces

The magic idle windy spaces
alone had not touched
the goat. Ah, soft, a good autumn
advances.
A corner, with his own, somewhere
softly meets.

At the center of their fingernails,
unquestioning
before,
privacy changes.

Rebirth

If I could be born an animal;
if I could shed like a snake;
shed my used tongue;
call softly in one Noun
out of her place
a Woman who would exaggerate nothing and who would bend
    down often,
hushing the flesh-eater known as Literal Knowledge
that the animal inside the animal might immediately
rejoin its Body;
if I could make a Wife out of the womb I stepped from,
of the slim-hipped tissue stepped from
make her;
call softly together the Bride's many-fused tongues,
and grasp them,
and put each of them in my mouth and suck them;
if I could be born again in my own Body
at last:
many-skinned; naked; quick; freshly-spoken.

STAN RICE

The Pier in Berkeley

I am at sea, sort of. The slime is coral. Some idiot's
campfire has burned a hole
in the wooden pier
as round as a man's screaming-out. Boy
it is old. Moss like a woman's hair
grows from the pylons, rises and falls:
but she hangs on. She has to. The earth is her head.
You look down through the silvery-edged opening
and there is the water: a piece of black marble
worked over with an axe.
It moves but it stays right there.
You wish you were inland. Your girl
outstretched, hooked through the cheeks,
her hair floating straight up
over the seat-covers. That salt
was so sugary. Come
back.

Incoming tide;
stretched shine and foam over rocks;
silvery lumber;
a porpoise that looks like it swam into a boat's propeller
lies on the sand,

one clean slit three-fourths the length of its body,
guts pooching like cake icing.
Should you enter?
Must. cant. Must. cant. Must. Entering

that drained girl, inland, ribs
like a ladder under snow, wish-boned, buttocks
slit by a nearly white shadow,
comes back. Boy
it was simple. Better
to be at this black hole burned in the wood by some idiot's
        campfire;
scream-hole, scream-hole;
deep as your mother.

Autumn

The glass tells. The wood
that keeps the window the window
tells. We are near Fall. Outside
a branch is being skinned: its true: the meat
is much much redder than the cow.
The clumsily slaughtered leaves tell
we are falling. Now
comes Later.
The trees walk on fire. The Flood
stumbles.

The Power

The water ticks in the flowerbed.
Wine.
It makes the page move unnaturally. Tonight

think of Savonarola, he looked like an ape,
his cowl, the smooth woven hair
of his eyebrows, very black, but

he was a powerful man: heretic, dope, he burned,
the wild burn, and as I listen
to this rainfall making nipples in the mud

what power, I wonder, what power
makes the mad-of-tongue (even Joe McCarthy was one)
be so seized that everything goosesteps after?
A leak in the cortex.

That I should want to go out now
(admittedly drunk)
and drop face down and suck the nipples in the flowerbed
. . . that it should actually nourish me,

that acting like a tree I, a man, should not become a tree
makes the world unnaturally vulnerable.
Each woman-woven language ends on this:
power to be loved, to suck, to strangle on it.

On the Murder of Martin Luther King

1. The young Texan reads a book.

Each night has new meaning
in it. Tonight. Aeschylus, I hear your black and gold masks
thunk in the yard, where each leaf of ivy
comes up,
reaching and sparkling.

Its like a . . . like a . . . party:
the terror hosting the terror hosting
the tendrils. They are white,
their strength coils through the black yard like
a snake around a chicken egg
it swallows without breaking.
Gold souls in fragile things: Im watching the stars
in the black branches and Im thinking of the meaning

this man's death has.
If it will last.
If any.

Its April.
The guests in my garden
stick out their white tongues under the dirt.
Light will give them color.
It changes the complexion of the mask.
Aeschylus, I hear in my brain rather than in my ears
your deathmask clink against the gravel.

This night means I am in it
up to my lips. Kick me.
I am beginning.

He stuck his head up
because the hero is always more visible. Or rather,
he was a hero and therefore his head
stuck up above the sludge we call the flow we live in.
BANG!   Aeschylus, you said:
       God marks that man with watchful eyes
       Who counts his killed by companies;
       And when his luck, his proud success,
       Forgets the law of righteousness,
       Then the dark Furies launch at length
       A counter-blow to crush his strength
       And cloud his brightness, till the dim
       Pit of oblivion swallows him.
But this is not a literary poem.
I am aware that this is a Poem.
I am singing but I am sinking
into the little black hole
in Martin Luther King's black jaw.
Or, as one of his friends put it: "His face just exploded."
The language got too much.
His life stopped working.

So what is a dead Greek to this dead nigger?
The blackest thing about me is my sexual hair.
At the Vice-President's fund raising dinner where the news
came out the Chaplain said:
    "The King is dead, long-live-the-King-of-Peace-on-Earth."
Meaning: each night has new meaning in it.
Meaning: we have heard that soft language before and it grew
    white ivy.
Meaning. I am. My black roots are hair; are
    showing.

2. The young Texan sees the children with the crushed souls
for the first time.

Suave children black and brown
stand in my ivy patch
knocking on the openings in bottles
with their palms.
Standing in the wide leaves
each still an ear of dew
making the bottles sound like
they are grief stricken. Children without real eyes
in their heads I think
standing in my ivy patch
if I struck their faces with my palm lightly
would thunk like bottles
so pure is their emptiness.

The physical world around them a mystery,
no lit animals,
no yellow,
just holes in their faces. The ivy is more human.

Give them many bottles,
wet their lips with Coke,
suave black and brown bodies full of echoes,
scary as Death in the ivy standing
knee-deep in the green ivy,
beating on the mouths of bottles with their palms,
grieving and smiling.

3. The young Texan returns to the Texas State Fair and sees
the source of his racism sitting in a glass cage over a tank of
water.

And here is where the niggers wash.
You can kill a nigger at last.
You can throw a baseball at the target hooked to his body.
Now you can pay him back for his sensual blackness.
You can drown him and drown him but still
he will laugh like a sleek, stupid ape,
because that's what he is.
Sleek; shiny; the whites of his eyes are yellow;
the brown pupils covered with a mucous blue film;
the teeth. You can make his seat snap open
and down into the white filthy water he drops,
his big black hands and feet mixed in the foam,

staring at you through the glass tank
like an animal that you cant kill,
you cant kill him,
he keeps rising all oily and fresh, like a seal,
taunting you, virile, soiling you, soiled, your victim,
    your master.

4. The young Texan re-reads a book.

Agamemnon's slit jaw on the floor's Lord blooms
like a beautiful idea about freedom.
My vacuumed room will not grow ivy.
April to it is merely a season.
So *what?*
So let the ears of ivy hear me knocking
on my ears until the crackle
of gunfire forces a bloodred rain from the thunder.
Im sure that Agamemnon's golden death mask is a fake.
Martin Luther King's skin is awake in my garden.
It talks.
It says: your uncle's, your father's, your brother's, your own
bones bones bones
are pale and rotten and crushed and swallowed.
The little black hole in his cheek
sprouts water. Tonight.
I see.
I am.
My own.
Skin's father.

FLOYCE ALEXANDER

The Lotus Eaters

(homage to Martin Luther King, gunned down, Memphis, 4 April 1968)

This is the dance America wanted! the dance of death.
The small animals come out of the ground,
Nothing left of them but their skins and shells,
Saying: Americans, kill what you can't
Understand.
            Sirens! Yellow fire-trails!
The year of the lean wolf stalks America,
Eats its own entrails, devours its children.
Immolation of the children of Asia.
Ambush of the ghost of Guevara in Bolivia.
And now our Gandhi, holed up in Memphis,
Taking a breath of air, leans back on the hotel
Balcony, all the sky, a southern calm, slow drawl
Of clouds, filling his eyes, before lightning cracks:

Red-necked, corpulent, born diseased, man-snake
Twisting its scaled body through narrow clefts
In the hills,—white man! who knows how to murder,
And does, the dark-skinned man, a tattoo of bullets
Against the rough-cut cross of his body,—a lesson,
They said, chewing persimmons, spitting snuff,
            drinking red-eye,
Vagrants of spittoons, my father, uncle, grandfather,
            rifles
Slung over their shoulders, leaving home, glum,
            ready to hunt down deer.

Aphrodite

This is Jacqueline's

I

'a brown, black-spotted butterfly'
sailing through meadows to old men
trapped in cities

lights beside your knee
trails you through the door
takes you to her lair to love

eyes beautiful as blue clouds
she likes that greasy slap of sex
the branch between her thighs

just born and she can do it to
anyone any time who wants
to catch her heart in a net

II

I was an old man trapped in a city
She a young mare from Red Bank New Jersey
Wearing her hair cropped, her fingernails sharp
Overweight with calluses on both heels
Bra-cupped breasts 36-D, hips 50
The smell of her skin like rancid butter
Tibetan holy men would die for her
Yak juice oozing from her body's deepest valley

I found I could sing on her instrument
While she was talking on the telephone
She made no conversation more than once
She came to see me in the city twice

Li Po

He said how much he had died for the sake
of a poem. It was not much: his hand
quivered, and his body shook in its shell.
The river whispered goodbye, and darkness
began crouching in the shade of the hills.
He rose from the mud and walked upriver,
writing his large letters full of sadness
with the edge of an empty wine bottle.
Water trembled and spread in crystal fans
along the shore, swallow-tailed butterflies
sipped from the heavy place where he had sat,
a dark woman splashed happily downstream.
A tiny white moth hovered around him.
The sun opened and closed its sleepy eyes.
Two dogs sniffed his tracks for a scent of food.
A child wandered, crying, thorns in its hands.
Wings spread from the shoulders of the mountain.
He was writing about his memory
of how it had been once in the city,
pockets stuffed with money, and one woman
kissing his ear, turning a dark corner.

He swung his head around once,
his eyes deep amber stones against the glare,
his arm rocking the bottle in an arc
over the foamy bones of his poem.

Nowhere

Can you see the bird coming through bushes
To this small clearing where I am loving
You and loving every part of the land
Where we lie and come together and writhe . . .
I could see his tail less than twenty feet
Away, erect, a stick growing up, out
Of the broken land, as I watched you move,
Your breasts boiling in the heat of the shade,
Your thighs turning to gold in a cauldron,
The red fever of your lips, and your cries
I heard echoing through this universe,
Eve screaming when she was ripped from the rib
Of a man who looked like me: his cock hard
And plunged deep as it would go into grass,
While his bloodshot eyes kept watching the bird
Hopping tail-high in the grass, in frenzy
And future knowledge that this, too,
Would come alive, this meadow where
The bird watched us fucking the world to birth,
Then, once we were done, rose into the air.

Guerrilla

for Margaret Randall

Huddled in your house,
your friend's bright red fingernails
throw sparks
as she gives the news:
Díaz Ordaz is closing the gas stations!
A day in Mexico City.

In a month the world will change,
violets humming in the breeze
of loaded bombers

whose tiny blue targets are painted in my dreams
with visions of Betty
one winter night stepping out of her panties.

I remember her
here
a year ago writing our name
in blood
across the face of our single shadow
struck against the cold stone of the Zócalo.

Tanks rumble through the squares of Prague,
through the plazas of Mexico City,
bayonets fixed in the streets of Chicago.
When I return
her closet's half full and the house empty,
cold as a lamb losing its first wool.

The rusty gate is opening.
Are the granaderos coming?
The life between my legs
has never given birth.
I have a machete in the car.
The gas still flows.

September 1968

FLOYCE ALEXANDER

Poem for a Painter

Compare needles to the shrewd injectors of the State:
A poisoned porcupine dead in the road,
Run down by a one-armed night-blinded veteran
Who counts the birds he leaves sprawling behind him;
Not enough living things have fallen from the sky.
Another man who fights wars in his head
Remains aloft. Puncture his spread arms, doctors,—
Mendicants of eighteen years of our lives,—
And he drops with deflated flaps of skin at his sides,
Plummeting to another sky that turns all ice.
May conservationists take him for a murdered bird,
Then turn, faces strung together like beads,
Reach out and make a perfect capture of themselves.
One-armed in your nineteenth year, sit out the sun,
Become an owl flapping through the burnt shape of the moon.
'Soon there will be nothing left alive above ground,'
You say, leaning your body down canyons;
'I paint what it means for a tortoise to live.'

An Artist Paints Dawn

It is red
like the tears of mother
and gold as the spinning earth
beside her grave.

There's the river in its distance,
brown as god.

But no,
he looks again, as artists must—
the charcoal breath of fathers
blocks his view.

What We Remember

Whispers of the wheatfields
searching night

Brooks half-hidden where
our pebbles skipped

The pickers and their shadows,
heads bowed as if to pray
(we thought each was a god then
and still do)

The whispers of the wheat
where others learn.

The Maiden

With a sadness curtained
Windows
  Left behind

She steps along a beach
Abandoned now

And with a stick left by a
Wave
  Protesting still

Upon sands she knows must
Wander

Scrawls her name.

ROCHELLE RATNER

Yellow Apples

Brooding,
their faces seem to shrink
on branches that will never
know a god

But this season's a blistered
hymnal

to be fingered page by page.

Migrant Workers

Digging,

spade and sun will mock
your muffled thirst

But as you stumble westward
. each alone .
let the roots of ancient
farmers

be your sleep.

On the Death of Theodore Roethke

The papers say he died in a swimming pool,
but that's not the way that poets go.
A poet's exit is terrible: as his hour
approached the wind began to blow,
rattling the windows of his study.
Below the lake shuddered; fish grew still.
Above the light soured like spoiling grapefruit.
He listened and heard the awful rupture
of petals and stems and a chorus of worms
singing in the compost. He laid down his pen
and went out, feeling the weight of his flesh,
sensing his time of singing was done,
he who had turned the world into honey.
And he moved through his garden like a heavy bee,
his dark suit gathering a bloody pollen.

From: Three for Robert Bly

2

In Minnesota the barns are black
against the snow;
there is a muffled, sickening sound
of blows to the heads of cattle.

In barn doorways and lofts
men whose mission it is to clear the state
of everything personal or strange
glance at luminous watches. Some

wait for the poet to step out into the night air.
They will freeze his body in cross hairs sights,
and each rifle has an infrared device
for tracking souls in darkness and snow.

A Gothic Tale

There is a TOP SECRET room in the White House
filled with the carcasses of horses, dogs and snakes.
At midnight the President's favorite darky
entertains him with a soft shoe;
then he unscrews the President's head
and wraps it gently in Saran Wrap.
Humming "Old Black Joe," he collects the heads
of the Vice President, the Secretary of State
and the Secretary of Defense
and then takes them to the secret room
to soak in the compost.
The heads, renewing themselves,
make noises like giant slugs.

The Great White Father

Engineers
found the Great White Father dying,
caught in a fish ladder at the Dalles.
He wore a rubber mask
that disguised him as an Indian grandmother
and his last words were
"I want to be loved!"

After two centuries of massacring
salmon and buffalo on the dark river floor
he had tried to climb to the light.

The medicine man who was summoned
to sing for the Great White Father's shadow
had a vision of it slipping down river
towards Portland,
bloated with ears and testicles
and human hair.

Marian at Tassajara Springs

1

I remember your hair
spread out like black moss against the rock,

your skin tasting faintly sulphurous
from the mineral baths,

your laughter like a spring
swelling up

from the lime and chalk of your pelvis
and flowing out the white stones of your teeth.

I caught the small trout of your tongue
in my mouth.

2

It was October.
The Monarchs were dying,

falling through the air
like the acorn leaves

and landing on the rocks and stones
where they would rest,

slowly moving their faded
orange and black wings

as if they were trying to fan themselves
back into flame.

We talked of the certain end
of our season

as the crumpled ghosts of old lovers
floated past us on the water,

and of something waiting
in cities and in each of us

that is hostile to love
and to rocks in clear streams.

I will think of that day
and the wings of your shoulders

when the firestorm comes
and the wind

whips my shirt
to black ash and orange flame.

Freeway

An infected vein
carrying filth to and from the city;

a funnel
draining a huge operating table.

Even the light here
is the color of pus.

All the late models
have tinted windows to shield the murderers

and the chrome is honed
to slash and carve.

The city has complied
by drawing a rubber curtain of shrubbery

to enclose the view
and muffle the screams.

A Hybrid Villanelle on a Line of Li Po

Drunk on the moon, a sage of dreams,
I offer the mountain a shot of bourbon
and I offer you a shot from the hip.

The last full moon I called you on the phone,
drunk on the moon, a sage of dreams,
and talked to a cloud your ear.

Tonight clouds move across the moon
and I write this poem by candlelight,
drunk on the moon, a sage of dreams.

Drunk on the moon, a sage of dreams
I pick up the phone to dial your hair
but the line is dead, the mouthpiece a crater.

Two moths have snuffed out in the candle flame.
Drunk on the moon, a sage of dreams,
my moth heart crackles in the lunar fire.

You are probably making love tonight,
giving your monk rice wine from the hip.
Drunk on the moon, a sage of dreams,
I piss a bloody wine in the moonwhite dust.

Days

My week-days pile in me like dirty clothes.
The door is locked. Is this inside or out?
I keep my Sundays empty as my house.

I Edgarize my hours, towels, nose.
I have ten fingerprints all of my own.
My week-days pile in me like dirty clothes.

Where heavy chairs stood once in repose,
The little lizards do their push-ups now:
I keep my Sundays empty as my house.

I love the way you talk, so well-composed:
Your words are like a napkin on my mouth.
My week-days pile on me like worn-out clothes.

The curtains hang like curtains: from their toes.
I write these verses Monday, almost now,
But keep my Sundays empty as my house.

I've lost the breath to say my yes-and-no's.
Between these words the paper sings aloud.
My week-days pile in me like dirty clothes.
I keep my Sundays empty as my house.

Icons

Change
compels me more
than responsibility
for change.

.

one separates two

.

middle
shared

.

EYES

unity of spirit
behind
duality of form

.

Holding
the two ends
you hold it
by the middle.

.
ends
bend

.
A net
between
the players.

.
The seed goes
outside me
inside you.

.
contact
makes
sound

.
The mother bears
the son
that bears the penis.

.
At its peak
it expels
what sleeps
at its core.

.
The whole belongs
as part
of its without.

.
Shadow inside light
echoes darkness
outside light.

.
Perceiving inside
the outside
of everything else.

.
Leading out
your body opens
for father and son.

.
Reflection of the flame
on the wax it melts.

.
If you loved your dead
you would eat them.

.

First
the surface
hardens.

.

Freer
behind
the mask.

.

Burdened
with what
he is not.

.

Coming to trust
something in the past
he didn't have.

.

It takes us
where we want to go.

.

We build the house of respect
to keep the guest of love.

.

nothing holds
water together

.

air	air	air
earth	water	earth
earth	earth	earth

.

Centrifugal
water slides down
the convex surface.

.

Down the concave surface
water slides
towards the center.

.

away
from the center
it multiplies

.

All
that is given up
remains.

Neighbor

The Polish superintendent snores behind the wall.
A sailor gone super, this man
can ride a pint of Gallo like a tide
to any slanting whore beyond the Burman Sea.
He never quite made the change of life.
Some wineless night, the cock too hard
and windless for the East,
he'll either blow his pipes against the wall
or learn to buccaneer a neighbor's wife.
He would sing to her:
  My radiators, cold at these late hours,
  will whisper heat
    for your wet lingerie and rayon flowers.
This Polish motherfucker owns a key
to every door in the building.

SANDFORD LYNE

The Guest of Our Lovely Daughter

the family takes me in
on the recommendation of their daughter
the rights privileges and possessions of the family
are accorded me
the family takes me in
no more hunger cold heaviness
how could they know how destitute i am
on the recommendation of their lovely daughter
they give me hot food my own towel a bed with deep quilts
they ask if i want anything put in the wash
they give me the key to the bookcase
they show me the place where the liquor is kept
they show me the intricacies of the hi-fi
on the recommendation of their delicious daughter
they go to work
they give me a key so i may let myself in and out
they leave me with their daughter sweet as lobster steaks
how could anyone know how destitute i am
they give me their daughter so i may let myself in and out
she says i am mistaken
she goes into her bedroom and closes the door
i hear her stockings rubbing against each other
as if this were a movie
i hear the music on her small hi-fi
i feel cold

how could i know how destitute i am
i drink the liquor they have accorded me
i go into the room of their lovely daughter
        on my own recommendation
i go in up along her stockings
with my hand over her mouth
she stops struggling
she stops breathing her heart stops
i lock her in the bookcase
her mother and father return from work
i poison their drinks i smile at them
their hearts stop
i put them in their bed
i lock that room
how could anyone know how destitute they were
i have taken the family in

Notes from an Ohio Tavern

1.
In taverns,
There is a rituality in the careless talk,
The nostalgia of heavy animals
Driven from caves and nests,
Sitting on fence posts in bare, moonless fields.

2.
The Negro at the counter nods
In his draft of Black Label,
Then blows smoke into an empty bottle.
What was it his mother told him, years ago?

3.
White-headed babbler in a booth:
He remembers a snow that fell all night
Through the eaves of his attic room.
It was a foot high on his quilts by morning.

4.
So many here tonight!
The jukebox sings in voices

They all can imitate.
It tells them they are loved.

5.
The high school coach
Who can no longer arouse enthusiasm in boys:
His hand rests on the basketball-kneed woman
Who cheers his victories
And forgets his losses.

6.
It is closing time,
And the snows drift in the shadowless streets.
They will walk home, or drive,
Moving like beavers
In black water
Under ice
Toward huts of sticks.

Poem for a Selfpitying Friend/ for Lost Loves

It is over, it is
life
burning out, only now
you have been permitted
to feel
its
sore flame. Look in your mirror,
say *Loser.*
Scum off the dried
material of her kiss.
It is life, the burnt offering of it,
it is
a
pilgrimage, give
your heart
like a stone to the wind's wonderful
drill.

253

Home-Made Peach Ice Cream

Smoke-eyed lover, mouth
smeared with irresistible fruit, hair
bleached to the bone,
patched traveler
in yoke,
in underwear bearing
the skidmarks of my rectal disasters,
I have pissed into the tin hole
of the book of women
in a hundred sordid towns.
There, in graffiti,
in words barred
           and soldered together
like second-hand headboards of Hollywood beds,
I hear my name repeated: kid, poet, pig, my best . . .

One struggle is finished:
we are prone
to be the bodies of ourselves, rising
on struggling frogkicks
in the light of God,

      beamed up,

         gigged!

So, but for this quaintly ribbed flesh, puffed
organs of oozing brown
and spitting
purple, residue-makers, under the sail of skin,
this transporter of riches, plasma
and odors, belly-hold of shitloads
from the world's markets,

and intricate Arabian urinary
pipeline
laid inobtrusively in
along the dazzling, hot folds,

we would be two mating boneheaps, mantis-
fossil in the tall dying grass,
bone on bone on
bone in the evaporating rock.

Star-gaze Poem

In whatever galaxy,
I believe there must be creatures like ourselves,
dreamers,
savages,
poets,
builders of canoes,
far-scattered eyes moving
against the twinkling darkness of the heavens,
pilgrims
in equivalents of dust,
singers of small laments:
the ones we also know,
so well.

So,
for one such as me
this earth is enough of the possibility of grace.

I step out on my small porch, gaze:

these tiny lights, these beacons, bobbing
so far away in the night
we
cannot hear their bells
marking
the shallows of the universe.

The Dog

The old, shade-baked dog bolted
off the porch,
the plowboys in a beat-up Chevy yelling
like wet flags, a towel
wrapped in the hubcap.   By the time
the dog caught up, he looked
like an enraged sud, running on stilts.
With a mercy that expects greater gore
the boys held off
the acid-gun from his eyes.
His snarling teeth
clinched in on the towel, took the bait,
took on
down his whole length the spin
of the tire, like
a woodstock on a lathe, his head
wrapped turban-fashion like a splayed
Saracen.   He felt every bone
snap and puncture
some inexpendable organ,

even for a dog.

When the towel worked loose
from the bloody
ornament of the smoking wheel, he did
not convulse or yelp,
or die.   But standing
kneedeep in his dropping guts, he took
the middle
of the road, and waited.
When the car turned around, came back
in a whine, he
planted himself like an iron
pick, met the grill
face to face, sent
his whole insides up the hood, the windshield, like
the world's biggest butterfly, blocked
the entire vision
of the onrushing earth, the shoulder,
ditch,
telephone pole, the
falling sky

in the kingdom of dog.

A *Change of Heart*

Antlers of a buried intelligence
I would have called you,
nerve ends of the Earth
cracked through to hear me now
this evening say forgive me, Mr. Tree—
there's nothing left between us.

Once you bolstered the sky for me,
I deliquesced up through your arms
and sucked the heavens dry.
We were the sum of incidence,
consumers of every meaning.

We've dreamed too much!
and dreamed away the sticks and stones.
From branch to twig,
thoughts rarefy and lose their heads.

In the Garden

I said I'd let life battle it out
like real life and let the weeding go—
now look, spuds sunk, my beans cashiered,
five rows of seedlings, missing, presumed dead—
what a failure! a frail platoon
of jaundiced, nude cornstalks is all that's left;
and who's to say who's at fault; it was
surely a death wish on both of our parts.

Now the pumpkin climbs the grape arbor, flourishes,
then falls—a fatal concussion. And smell,
the onions and mint patch seed the air—
it's a crazy salad we breathe! and a battle
just breathing. Should I prune the day back,
gas the cats, turn my poems loose—or what?
Must I kill to live? or let live?
I'll move to an apartment, keep goldfish.

And here, friend Steve's washed, dispensable face
stops in for a beer—I'm thinking,
will he die in his black Volkswagen? or live
to perish like the carrots, getting
only dirt to stick to his ribs?
Is life a moral drama, I wonder,
or merely the weather? and offer him chips.
Who planted you under a drainspout, Steve?

With me it was spores in the peach fuzz,
a costly pubescence—my fix
when I hit the black earth, blushed
like a radish and perished from chagrin.
I remember pitiful pink shades,
the bruised frowns of genitals—confusing flesh.
It's a crazy salad, so terribly
serious and all the time foolish, like sex.

And who wins? I'm dead, my life an object
I collect on shelves, on paper, a choice retrospect—
or I live, regardless as a cucumber's green.
One death means nothing; we're costive or loose
and either way we're addling
over what it all meant. It's crazy,
but where's escape? One life is nothing too—
not us, we're only a passing mood.

PETER FELLOWES

Predator

—for Elliott Coleman

Landscapes are all we get

the barest line of a hill
thwarted by a house

this cloud not really very like
the whale, just cloudy

all we get is the tree
black, green, and windblown till it falls

four elements
agenda

and this bird from nowhere
sent by no one
auguring nothing

this bird
who brings the taste of meaning
naturally as flight, or seed
he later eats

we stalk you in our sleep.

Hero and Holy Man

Who paid his way in flesh sticks
through the world
like so much wampum
traded for the light of day
and saw it inexplicably each time
in place upon his forehead
and nonetheless bore onward—where else?

Who saw them dead
walk right up to him
and let him know how they felt
and let them drink,
hearing them out,
till he got out of there,
and didn't let it get him down.

Who fought phantasmagoria
with humans on their breath,
black-livered gods, and lived
to kill the wickedest of men
and still sleep well

beside his handsome wife.
He did this.

Who might have bellyached
to taste those holy breasts
until his cheeks at last
did pouts, flopped out and breasty
and he spouted senseless words
of hidden and dark meaning,
missing all this other stuff.

Quick witted, quick!
whose teeth would soften, slush,
his eyes turned yellow over
while he ruminated thus,
he gumming out his poems,
"O light, O dolorous light,
there is no goodness in us!"

View from an American Window

On a rainy day, a sky
a child might water color,
letting his feelings out and run together
in purples from the pavement up—

But here, you've seen the clichés before,
these people too laundered, and earnest,
this corner too busy, too lonely later.
Your face isn't face, Mr. Person,
no kidding: the trees don't grow in bouquets,
they shriek, tearing their hair out.
A face doesn't look like a face.

You want to paint yourself in
in dangerous, cooked-alive reds,
a brilliant crustacean! Do.

Across the world, for peace,
the ignorant armies are clashing,
clashing with Maryland, with windows,
with Matthew Arnold's despair.
Day curls in our hands, brave hearts!

Cold Waltzes

Twirled down the years
dizzying the sleet,
our fingers blue and touching.

No music thawed
the arctic smile—
that gash our faces wore.

Were quill stiff spines
in the ballroom world,
ah, such cold waltzes.

Unaware that Avessek . . .

Berries on the outwash plain,
mudflat, esker, hole
and swamp
enclose the summer
he clings to
like a dozing lemur
in the croft of a tree.

Wrinkling the image
of drenched pines,
their peaks in the river,
he leaps
in the water,

unaware that Avessek,
Pharaoh of the North,
commands the ice
to go southward,

that,
outmost at the Arctic Pole,
cold sabres gash
a trembling sun.

Sauerkraut Talk Shreds in His Ear . . .

Sauerkraut talk shreds in his ear;
the night supine and breaking wind.
Chekov's "Life is cabbages and quarrels"
comes to mind
and how years growled
in time's distended stomach.

Flo at the end of the table
riffling through old recipes,
how her titties once were snow peas,
hair buttery, pepper-firm ass . . .

even the world was firmer
when they rolled through escaroles of summer
curled in the heart of the leaves.

COLETTE INEZ

The Woman Who Loved Worms
(From a Japanese Legend)

Disdaining butterflies
as frivolous,
she puttered with caterpillars,
and wore a coarse kimono,
crinkled and loose at the neck.

Refused to tweeze her brows
to crescents,
and scowled beneath dark bands
of caterpillar fur.

Even the stationery
on which she scrawled
unkempt calligraphy,
startled the jade-inlaid
indolent ladies,
whom she despised
like the butterflies
wafting kimono sleeves
through senseless poems
about moonsets and peonies;
popular rot of the times.
No, she loved worms,
blackening the moon of her nails

with mud and slugs,
root gnawing grubs,
and the wing case of beetles.

And crouched in the garden,
tugging at her unpinned hair,
weevils queuing across her bare
and unbound feet.

Swift as wasps, the years.
Midge tick and maggot words
crowded her haiku
and lines on her skin turned her old,
thin as a spinster cricket.

Noon in the snow pavilion,
gulping heated saki,
she recalled Lord Unamuro,
preposterous toad
squatting by the teatray,
proposing with conditions,
a suitable marriage.

Ha! She stoned imaginary butterflies,
and pinching dirt,
crawled to death's cocoon
dragging a moth to inspect
in the long afternoon.

COLETTE INEZ

For Denise McNair
    (bombed in Birmingham,
    Alabama, September 15, 1963)

Testified that Miss McNair
on an Alabama Sunday
in the colored church,
the reverend saying:
"evil and good share
God's light"
when the pews blew up,
walls caved, ceiling crashed,

did hereupon
plunge down
to the brown earth
having learned her testament;
the meek inherit dust.

Slumnight

T.V. gunning down
the hours
serves as sheriff
in a room
where one yawn
triggers off another,

sends time scuffling
into night.
Wars slugged out
on vacant lots
sign an armistice
with sleep.

Turned to a wall,
the children dream
and the moon pulls up
in a squadcar.

Force of Snow

What went out
of the house
(refuse, smoke,
fumes of roast,

a hausfrau love
for placed things),

that ice grips
the mansard roof
contracts the frame
of a wizened door?

Inside, cold to colder
fires,
soil the grate
she scrapes for heat.

The mansion's lady
sets the clock
to ring on summer;

green caved in
on porches,
pine branch sawing

down the light.

No hounding love
kept at bay,
howling rage
held back.

The force of snow
on the house, a weight
of dimming sense.

She hears her mind
unwinding
music from a dented horn

and lets things
come to rot.

An Exchange of Letters On
Suicide Porpoises

> It was with horror that I read in the New York
> Times of April 23 a news report that Navy
> scientists have trained porpoises, carrying explo-
> sives in body harnesses, to ram enemy subma-
> rines. . . . How can anyone engage in securing
> the confidence of such especially friendly crea-
> tures as porpoises and then plan to shatter them
> to bits?
> —ASHLEY MONTAGU

I

Dolphins Rampant

No longer do they romp out to sea
with our liberty tucked away
in the lower instincts.
They are explosive now, half human
and skillful as a fine circuit.

Floating for years on the bottom,
our submarines have grown gills.
Their crews, all memories of land
fading, are pink as entrails.
They do not need any light
but their ghostly sonar, or health
while the torpedo tubes are clear
of tumors.
                On land,
wandering now and then into our bodies,

we feel our sluggish limbs
float in the air; and play,
the fugitive, comes home
to a false pardon. We are waiting,
our heads above water,
with jobs to do. Aimless
as children, we are all armed.

> Porpoises are no doubt especially friendly crea-
> tures, but has Professor Montagu never tried
> making friends with a draftee? —B. F. SKINNER

II

Furthermore . . .

. . . we have plans to train tigers
in a unique rage for the finer things.
Elephants with a sense of property
will stamp out brushfires,
squirrels bearing sly diseases
will nest in the collectives. Their brains
will be little radios
to rally the longing kulaks.

WILLIAM BROWN

Freedom forever in the Animal Kingdom!
They will consort with our agents
for nothing. We'll give up meat
and eat grass out in the fields
and the seals will be our coast guard.
We'd let them be, like women
and the old—we have dogs of our own
at home, and goldfish—
we'd do it ourselves, with our bare
teeth and hands, but the Beast
is everywhere, and we are so few.

Man in the Street

His mouth is open,
his fingers trail in the gutter.
I can't make out if he's
drunk or dead. And of what?

It will be necessary
to touch the strange skin
of his wrist, peel back the lid
and look him in the eye.

If he had not fallen
here, I could be elsewhere,
forgetting my good name. That name—

it has made me a witness
who must administer first aid.
Dead man, rise up, go away.

Minding Our Own Business

Daily the rooms in which
it's safe to talk loud
get colder. The food gets worse
and our prettier women talk about leaving.

It wasn't so hard,
giving up our fiancés and cars,
with guns trained on our heads.
Indignant, our friends raised money

to help us stay. But we found it
safer to drop out of sight,
wait for the new moon
and sail off in small boats to get here.

Joking as we arrived,
we proclaimed festivals with floats,
queens and hard drinking to celebrate
the quiet victories we planned on.

Our houses were gay
as comic strips. Our music

was better than before, and cheaper.
Plainly the best talent got away with us.

But lately even those means
have dwindled. Aware that our chorus
is slurring its harder notes, the slickest
among us see through it all and gain admirers.

And yesterday, finding
the cellist from our string quartet
dead in his garden, his pockets full
but his throat slit, we imposed a curfew.

Meanwhile what spies we can afford
double against us
or vanish. And only they
can tell us what raids are planned

and which new
politicos mean trouble. For weeks
all we've heard from them
was a few numbers, circled invisibly

among the baseball scores
in yesterday's paper. After
ten seconds over a candle it came up
saying: "Freeze. The enemy is among you."

American Patrol

More on a mission
than a stroll, he finds the
Alley of Whiskers, where

his cohorts spread their limbs
like driftwood, halfway between
the two oceans.

The story will be how they
washed up here from the chic edges
of the land with lives

they tell like jokes. After
the men describe
sex with the bright and wiry companions

they dreamed would soothe their twenties,
the boys, lonely for their casernes,
name off the cheap

resorts of Italy and the dark cities
of the East
that they could not destroy. "She's hiding,"

say the men, "among her husbands."
"They drilled us," say the boys,
"for 30 months

"and warned us about spies,
but sent us home
unwounded. To hell with their cities."

Sooner or later
they come to deserts
where, years ago, they heard

the radio blast hours
of music to hide
the news from Washington and Pyong-yang

and girls
told them their futures. They
do not love their secrets.

For a beer
they tell all to the first
confidant. They ply him with hot

numbers in Rimini,
in Frisco, in Cannes. They tell him
how their guns worked, and why,

and, in the end, show deeds
to acres somewhere
none of them want to go.

Wondering How

Mine are the tactics
of the small burglar, watching
the statute run out
on his last haul.

I carry the passport
of the fabled horn of plenty.
Prices rise against me,
cigarettes get me down.
As I am bought and sold
by speculators, giddy
on my futures, I daydream
of imminent brotherhood.
The wisdom of Ben Franklin,
his French orgies,
his passion for himself
serve me as a soul.

I share with the world's peasantry
a wish for the big harvest
where I shall be both
green giant and hanged god,
reborn in the rice fields.
As the state rears
like a comic dragon,
spitting fire, I go
unarmed, with no leader.

The saintly assassins
break wildeyed into my solitude
and explain their plans.
I listen. I have yet
to enforce my will
on the home ground. I vote
by getting in the way.

GERALD BUTLER

Five Sections
From: *This Side of Orion*

Sancho Panza, someone has said, stands between Don
Quixote and God. The two men have two voices, arguing.
Cervantes, in his lucidity, his genius, resolved them into two;
but the Muse merges the two voices into one song. That song
constitutes what, in literature, we mean by Beauty.

1

Flash

The reason why all colors look deeper
when you're taking a walk after a morning
of making long love is because
it is later than you thought it was.

The reason why all colors look darker
is the twilight in the long muscles
you walk with to go buy eggs. One thing
that's everywhere is the night coming on.

The Great Nebula in Orion
even viewed with an opera glass envelops
the tip of his sword with a spermy haze
and in the winter the constellation hangs

over the black bucks of lower Berkeley.
They creep out of their ghetto
into Cadillacs to contemplate each other's

headlights in the all night drive-in restaurant.

These neighbors of mine see I am good to people,
to women, and so do not mind that I,
a white man, have, for religious reasons
and low rent, encroached on their district.

If you make love all morning, you
eat breakfast in the afternoon: but if
you're out early, you can also deepen colors
with sunglasses, since they are holy objects.

5

Malcolm X, talking to the City:

"Take a walk in my head
where dew could stroke your ankles
and where there are
names to give small animals
the rainbows
of whose invisible flight you hear.
You could hunt them perhaps
with the wide trees
of Africa around you

and with your dreams made of leaves,
of mud, of the sky between ruffled feathers,
all around you:
antelope would come.
The season for antelope would come,
filling the air with honor.
All breaths could be caught together
in the gathering and the fire
kept transparent by the stars.

Take a walk in my black head,
heave back the rainbow, hack
the plain to acres
till I spit all the dream out.
Breathe on the plain and burn it off
till I vomit up the shame
sweet as the dawn there is in hell
when the ghosts of the animals
pass through your white hands."

8

Winter
the cockroach
goes

into the cracks
and close to
the pipes.

Follow him.

11

Morphine combined with scopolamine is called
Twilight Sleep. The mother still feels the pain
but remembers nothing. Demerol and barbiturates
do the same thing. Though what they usually use
is spinal but not continuous caudal anesthesia,
a saddleblock, and this makes you feel nothing
but sharp pains in the diaphragm when he kicks.
Some of these I've even tried myself, once even
ate a tablespoon of belladonna, that deadly nightshade
they used to put in witches' brews: and saw

eucalyptus trees dance, cool silver leaved dykes
playing Mozart on their pianos until
a gang of migratory workers came
and set the hill on fire, outraged wetbacks,
and I started hitchhiking out of there.
I found the trees again, safe now
in the parking meters or telephone poles,
in anything tall, but the streets of those
farming California towns, Stockton where you could see
a Mexican house burn down

and the fire department not make it, the streets
were blockaded with piles
of terminal syphilitics, armless, legless, blind,
pimpled like me. It took such poison
to let me see flesh. One night
I smoked some marijuana and got so high
I couldn't tell which way the streets ran,
couldn't add, could barely understand
the speedometer numbers which was the only way
I could tell how fast I was going.

But I got home safe.
And put down drugs forever because
I'd found I was something, call it
just a pile of inhibitions, that would never get high,
that drove. And on my birthday,
for which you made me a cake, gave me
a pint of Hennessey and a notebook for my poems,
I came up to watch you eating the cake,
you not watching, a small boy in me came up
to my eyes. Sometimes when we make love
he comes and stands by the bed. Then I feel
lust. He has never touched you.
Proud girl who wept, who hated the pain,
I stood beside your bed
and kept trying to assure you, it's all right,
everything is going to be all right,
and thought to myself I would never touch you
again except tenderly. And then
your whole frame shook under the sheet
and the water broke.

12

But usually, words fill our heads, which we bring
close together while each of us keeps looking
to see if the other's eyes are still opened,
and when the kiss comes it's
another poem, speech, or bit of gossip.
And do you know what he said? He said
he'd paid a hundred dollars for Burns' novel course
and got nothing out of it, said, that Wayne Burns
is nothing but an egoist.
What did he want to hear?

Why flowers turn toward the sun,
or why, in New York City, they have a train
that goes sixty blocks without stopping
to get all the Negroes to Harlem in a bundle,
Clifford Brown, the great young trumpet player,
and I think Benny Goodman years ago
played a tune of it, "A-Train." Well,
for his hundred dollars
he wanted to know what flowers think
of subways, he wanted poetry, felt

in the questions that Burns kept raising
himself swelling up like a deep breath
and grew afraid, demanded poetry.
He wanted the classroom to be
a field of flowers, admittedly wildflowers,
but all turned toward the sun
which Burns refused to be.
Isn't it possible for a book to have
a scene that's not telling anything, not
trying to convince us? You can point

without preaching, say: take a look,
which is different from the way an advertisement
shows a product, from that showing
which is also a way of hiding.
In other words, can't we do something
more than lie? Music fills our heads,
blossoms into nothing, into this speechless hard
penis I have to love you with,
you who have opened to me
more than any flower can, you who are

more than any flower, more fragrant than
your skin I'll call a nigger, your woman's skin,
because I am not smelling you now, softer
than the petals you have between your thighs
because I am not touching them now,
you I am not trying to pierce now
or sell anything to, you who are swelling
beyond what I paid for you, woman I was afraid of,
wife I come in tonight.

To New Jerusalem

In 1846
the burning of Nauvoo
lit the sky with a ruin of light.
Brigham Young
drove his church
over the frozen river
and a wild continent
to his New Jerusalem.

They knelt in the snow
to pray for a prophet lost,
shot at Carthage, Illinois.
Darkness gathered in the cold
and hung in the branches
of dead trees,
in 1846.

Today,
driving over the plains
where the bones
of buffalo and Indian
enrich the soil,

I filled the belly of my mind
with wildflowers,
the ringing of lost bells
and white wagons,
gleaming beneath
the westward sailing sun.

I stopped
to mail a postcard
back to Salt Lake.
The ruin
of Omaha lit the sky
with a burning light.
I drive eastward,
into that fire.

DAN GILLESPIE

Poem for the Disappearing Bear

The bear
from the mountain
sits in a tide pool,
huge thighs spread
to wait upon death.
A garland of kelp loops his skull,
and a glittering mosaic
of crabs
hang and swing from his back.

Two squid,
suckered to a rock,
observe this incongruous monster,
only half-believing.

Beyond the white waves
heavy swells begin to build
and move from Asia.
The cold sea deepens.
Close your eyes, old bear.
There is nowhere else to go.
The dark waters
began on your green mountain.
They end here.

Above,
your Major Brother whirls away
in his ocean,
seven points of light
in search of a wilderness.

For a Bum Seen Walking the Rails

I stopped to watch you,
in mountain country in midwinter,
your jake-leg stumble
of old nightmares and dangerous gin
moving you as it will in the snow,
thirty years lost

losing count of invisible ties
beneath rails

and thought of my father
and pale girls
begging rides with the truckers
in 1933,
Chicago to St. Louis, New Orleans
or Amarillo.

I think of you
born to a country
where the crooked bone
could not endure, living out
a broken time,
kneeling over a fire
of rags and grease, watching
wind whirl the cold
through old trees

and my father's Oklahoma sun
darkening with dust,
you in salt sweat and frost
these thirty years

a river of crushed rock
flowing beneath your eyes,
now in this western snow
lost all these years
while America
found itself again in profit and chrome

and you jerking on crippled legs
down the rails,
blind in this whiteness,
still searching for your country.

Desert Gulls

When these inland gulls
swept down on fields black with crickets
the Mormons
thought them doves sent from heaven
to save their crops.

The green wheat took root,
ripened and turned pale in the sun.

Now the hills of wheat are gone.
No one remembers
that winter of Puritan endurance
when hunger was not yet history
and the gift of white birds.

Once, plowing a field
on a forgotten island
in the Great Salt Lake,
a flight of gulls
swirled out of a cloud
and settled on the broken ground,
thousands feasting in the furrows
I had made. I stopped the tractor
and standing in that field
felt the miracle moving again
that brought a prophet
and his people
to their knees
in a blizzard of doves.

Abandoned Copper Refinery

In rooms of stone
men thought these hills of slag
bright seed, black roots
gripping into a bedrock of profit.

Now the shell of the mill,
hollow as a worked out mine,
is silent
save for the chatter of birds
that nest in girders
under the sagging roof.
In a cold oven
two dogs growl and lock
in love.

Outside,
where the broken river
curves rich with the yellow sewage
of upstream cities,
on a mountain of black slag,
a lizard sleeps in the sun.

Strip Mining Pit

See where black water
slips down the broken spine
of rock,
down the ribs
of the hill, this stricken,
bony thing,
brown skeletal sprawl
stripped (efficiently),
by dragline
and digging rivulets of rain.
Rip it open
and the dark heart
gleams with promise,
with profit.
As thus, the prophet
sayeth,
lift your eyes
(to this wretchedness),
reach into
the rib cage,
grab a handful of heart
and run like hell.

Jasmine and the Gypsies

Jasmine sees intentions everywhere
She skates up the avenue
wearing shades she sees people through—
right inside
she reads a mind like ice

Circumstances
she says is what brought her here:
not like her will   On the bus
she formulates a truth bouncing
and forgets

Her brightest trait
is playing dumb   Unzipping a smile
with questions
men turn into wizards   For presents
they turn up Tarot cards

All her doctors are *out to lunch*
when she comes in
Twelve pairs of spectacles   pills   new teeth
is what she gets
She shaves herself between the legs.

2

It's not death honey
scaring me
but ahh I'm lost I really am   conscious
of being
not alone in that particular emotion.

One night I landed let's say
busted!
in jail   called to the king
of the gypsies
for a hand him being like a friend.

So what do you get?
Been stoned
by rain: a drop a sore   Not merciful!
So long thinking
the king ditched me   Dead

leaves blew in the park
She scuffs
chin up   hands pocketed she drops
on a bench
waiting to get lucky.

3

Today like every day waiting
she holds back
the shade   The radiator steams
like a train
She writes poetry

love poems to nobody!   Snow
on the streetlights
puts her in the Ice Capades
whirring solo
ballet on black ice for black eyes, nobility.

But shining
in the shower her poem changes
colors like her skin
I'm a walking globe from Africa
to Ireland . . .

Liveliest her nights when
she hangs
by the window of her dreams gawking
at forms
as human as words.

Two Shots: a Love Affair

Before

Will you love
come to bear
us together

unhappy children?
It will later
be like this:

I'll know how
I found you
till somebody asks.

After

Drinking
a long glass
of pain as purple

as grapes that stained
our lips
last summer

Drinking
ambrosial poison
I'll go on my way

disguised
as a child:
our own unborn.

The Corn Dance

1

She made her appearance at noon.
Soft bells jingled
like cotton
with drums; silver fox fur
sprigs of evergreen
on limbs soaked red for
the corn dance, August.

Her baby was stripped
of flesh
swaddled in furs and bells, rusted.
She heard through cotton
his small feet
on the soft dust pounding
and all his fathers calling oh.

Once she revived him
with yucca and gourd
or wild aster, his favorite blue.
Once she could feed him
sunflowers.
The sun was their forest;
she couldn't see the trees for the sky.

When the Spanish came
with laces, mosaics and knives
the white men entered
smiling.
With her mummified baby,
a broken dish,
under the Catholic altar
they hid like Jews.

Overhead people
ate caviar
their pale fingers stained black.
Fishbones, seashells stuck
in the vegetation
where she fell; her breasts dripped
to feel the skeletal teeth of her child
nip and swill.

2

Today
in thin ozone we turn
around and landscapes
attach
your hand to mine.
We walk on the ghost of the sea
in scratch and sun.

We go over
the evergreen mountain
our spirits high . . .
below, adobe walls
as angular as cows
are grazing
around a pockmarked skull.

The ocean just dropped
eleven thousand feet.
We can see the sun
set five times
by walking in circles down.
In the shade of aspens
we stop to smoke.

What a miracle
we are here both in the same year.
You might have stayed
in Spain.
Your camera
sees more than your eye, sensations
invisible; you know

you can't see pain.

The soles of our feet
are salted.
You know a baby's skull
and plankton
made this vegetation
what it is today.
Don't ask me why I feel like sand;
watch the dance.

I am a museum,
a zoological garden,
a room full of tourists,
a tourist full of rooms.
Oh and my heart
thumps
before this dance,
the rite of living bones.

To a Suicide

This was different
the way you might hear a sound
on the floor of a desert
or the heart just before sleep
    cabbage in its old sack
    holding everything . . .

    In the city
doors locked themselves
and the weakest buildings tremored
and clutched their addresses . . .
From the window the moon
blossomed in rows on your teeth . . .

Montana Visit

I

Bearded relatives I never knew
burrowed into the moonlike landscape
actually made things grow
and when it got better they
called out wives from the East
who ate potatoes and grew thick and
inarticulate each year dragging babies
from childhood as though childhood
were some kind of sickness.

The sons stayed scared by tradition
take stairs now one at a time
are stiff in the cities they visit
would rather walk than ride.
And their sons
live like businessmen from the town
cajole the same ground
their tools in bright colors
lace on their boots like
delicate instruments
kiss their thin city wives
and coax grain to grow in such
grade and quantity that it
bends the father in shame
like an old spoon.

Now I come here a visitor
foreign as the government
guilty as a sailor bringing back
a new disease.
It is my going that infects
will empty out their beds and chairs
transforming all their new machines
to old despairs.

II

Already there are
aunts in Seattle
cousins from Oakland
who never come back
except for funerals.

And there is evidence
from talk in the bars
that even the seasons may not continue
responsibly, may shift
and be lured by strange facts
of gravity
pulling the rains to the deserts of Nevada
or Mexico.

III

I have come back for reasons of desperation
to repay desperation.
I will be the stone, picked up and flung
and followed
as others followed what was flung
to this place.

Going will be given
by those who stay
and it will be taken by those who go
cautiously as the arms of mothers
teaching sons
to dance.

Dream Poem #1

I was driving north
in Canada
in a bus full of different friends from my life
was going north to fish
and I stopped along a huge lake
when we saw pieces of debris
hitting the water . . .
We watched . . . it was a plane, about to crash . . .
It wobbled and struck the water next to the shoreline . . .
I took off a heavy wool coat, my arms getting stuck
in the sleeves . . .
Lloyd Villet, a school friend,
followed me . . .
We swam to where the plane should be
dove down, the water warm,
lifted the craft by the tips of the wings,
took it up to the road . . .
It was suddenly diminished . . . the size of a toy . . .
I opened it and took out three tiny figures—a man
and two little boys . . . they were pink like plastic . . .
I pushed their small stomachs, water came out their
    mouths . . .
I breathed air down their throats, they became smaller . . .
They woke, lay wriggling in my hand
like baby mice . . .

317

Dream Poem #3

I had gone to see a fortune teller . . .
She was an old woman and she held my hand
for several minutes . . .
She said
"You're afraid, very afraid"
"You don't know who you are"
"You'll be with us a long time"

No One Can Be Trusted,
Something Tells Me . . .

My father is a strange man
who slides from his bed at night,
like a swimmer sliding into dark water,
    and floats off to meet the unheard sounds
       that cause dogs to go hysterical . . .
As he disappears from sight
his teeth glow with a soft uranium light
    and you can't make out his words . . .
      I think for years now he's been
having many sons
by beautiful, secret wives . . .

Thinking of Our Visits

Coming back and
coming back I am
watched by your children
whose eyes are green as
a Mallard's head
and you, blending smiles
with your medieval wife
and those Mexican girls you keep
dancing hysterically on your curtains . . .

Thinking of our visits
breaks panic from my blood at night
like a covey of pheasant . . .
This clock I own
now grinds me through its teeth . . .

I am boney as a knuckle
and sick of my mistakes
knowing even sidewalks keep themselves alive
with names and dates . . .

My friend, it's this: I'm sexless now
without the names of wife or child,
awkward as the piano
that sits
in a widow's house . . .

Undocumented Observations
from the Letters of G.

In the marrow of the living
families mourn their dead
and in their deepest parts
even greater families
mourning . . .

It's discovered
this has been going on
for some time now

in the simple arteries of ants

in the unsteady skulls of tortoises

making the bones dark and heavy . . .

This is best seen
when birds
are suddenly afraid
of falling . . .

Margaret

Upstairs in her room
  she gracefully dances
the newest dances
  with the tallest men . . .
staggers the air with perfumes . . .
chews bits of True Romance . . .
  adjusts her mirror . . .
sighs . . .

From where she lies
sandwiched in a garden
of printed sheets
  she swears once a week
she hears a man's breath
  leaking through the window
glimpses him flashing away
  from tree to tree . . .

A Poem About Baseballs

for years the scenes bustled
through him as he dreamed he was
alive. then he felt real, and slammed

awake in the wet sheets screaming
too fast, everything moves
too fast, and the edges of things
are gone. four blocks away

a baseball was a dot against
the sky, and he thought, my
glove is too big, i will

drop the ball and it will be
a home run. *the snow falls*
too fast from the clouds,
and night is dropped and

snatched back like a huge
joke. is that the ball, or is
it just a bird, and the ball is
somewhere else, and i will
miss it? *and the edges are gone, my*

hands melt into the walls, my
hands do not end where the wall
begins. should i move
forward, or back, or will the ball

come right to me? i know i will
miss, because i always miss when it
takes so long. *the wall has no*
surface, no edge, the wall

fades into the air and the air is
my hand, and i am the wall. my
arm is the syringe and thus i

become the nurse, i am you,
nurse. if he gets
around the bases before the
ball comes down, is it a home

run even if i catch it? *if we could*
slow down, and stop, we
would be one fused mass careening
at too great a speed through
the emptiness. if i catch

the ball, our side will
be up, and i will have to bat,
and i might strike out.

Quickly Aging Here

1.

nothing to drink in the
refrigerator but juice from
the pickles come back
long dead, or thin
catsup. i feel i am old

now, though surely i
am young enough? i feel that i have had
winters, too many heaped cold

and dry as reptiles into my slack skin.
i am not the kind to win
and win.
no i am not that kind, i can hear

my wife yelling, "goddamnit, quit
running over," talking to
the stove, yelling "i
mean it just stop," and I am old and

2.

    i wonder about everything: birds
    clamber south, your car
    kaputs in a blazing, dusty
    nowhere, things *happen*, and constantly you

    wish for your slight home, for
    your wife's rusted
    voice slamming around the kitchen. so few

    of us wonder why
    we crowded, as strange,
    monstrous bodies, blindly into one
    another till the bed

    choked, and our range
    of impossible maneuvers was gone,
    but isn't it because by dissolving like so
    much dust into the sheets we are crowding

    south, into the kitchen, into
    nowhere?

DENIS JOHNSON

The Man Among the Seals

—for Ed Schroeder

at night here in the park it is different:

the man by the seal pool stalks
through an acute emptiness, encircled
by the city. is he
taking off his clothes?

by day i have seen
the seals, enclosed, blundering
among the spattered rocks. they climb
like prisoners of a ferris wheel, above
their pool and above
the peanuts floating through
air, high over the sudden, too large

teeth of the spectators. but at night,
without their land-locked captors moving
gracefully by, the seals
seem less inept, even

on the hostile rocks.
before dawn they rise
and dive, becoming masters
in the water. the figure in

underwear on the left is not
a seal. before me and
an audience of trees he has
joined the seals. drunk, perhaps,

and, a staggerer on land,
perhaps he hopes to move cleanly,
like a seal, through water. or,
sober, perhaps he dives to assume
the clumsiness now shed by the seals: then
he will tumble drunk onto
the ground, and the seals, plunging

landward, will find
no awkwardness among the rocks, will
no longer wonder deep
within themselves at a dry hardness
which is not ice. each day

he will return, wetness
forever staining through his pants,
to watch his seals as they rise
above the rocks to pluck the floating

bits of food, as they slide through
the air over the trees, the
ferris wheel grown

stationary with shame, the tiny,
unfamiliar bodies jerking
under balloons through the lighted park.

DENIS JOHNSON

Checking the Traps

morning,
the door opening, changing
into a doorway. half

the night i stayed awake and smoked
and watched the mousetraps.
the mice were there, nudging
into cups and plates, one fell

into the toaster, but escaped.
they waited until i gave up and slept to die.
for these mice
the night will be long. i heard

the iron snapping
in my sleep and dreamed my wife was
closing the door.

two mice are dead, for my wife.
mice make her legs
go watery, as they do sometimes after her climax.

one mouse's head is barely
in the trap, one eye probing
toward the ceiling where i could tell him
there is nothing.
the other mouse is flung willingly under the iron

bar. i wonder, were they
married? was she pregnant? they are
going out together,
in the garbage this morning. it was
morning when we were married.
it has been morning

for a long time. that mouse, with his
eye. did he hear the iron snapping,
and dream it was his

wife with her stretching, laden tits
closing the door?

DENIS JOHNSON

In a Rented Room

this is a good dream, even if the falling is
no less real, and even if my feet will crumble

on the lurking ground. my throat itches, and i am
awake in this room which is no less vacant for

all my presence and there are no aspirin. here
is the sun with its tired surprise, the morning. there

are the cars and streets moving in the usual
fashion. the room wants to be rid of me. it must

fall open and communicate with other dim,
stifled rooms when i have slaughtered my body in

the sheets and fumbled streetward to soothe the itch. what
do you learn, room? what have you told, why are the stains

and the accusing glasses pointing so when i
return? there was the girl some time ago. *she* would

want to know where the guilt comes from, that hums over
the bed and descends, like an uncaring thumb, to

blot me out. she would help me, when the universe
has fooled me again, and the joke has gone too far,

when the itch, climbing, deep, remains after bottle
after bottle, and i inch toward death and i

must poke my body into a thousand vacant
darknesses before i strike the correct sleep, and dream.

ALFRED STARR HAMILTON

I was born in Montclair, N.J. I am 55 years old. I couldn't afford a formal education during the '30's depression. I have been on the road. I have been a hitchhiker through 43 states on no money at all. I am familiar with Salvation Army centers in that manner. I served (subservience) one year in the armed forces. I was A.W.O.L. I got a discharge somehow. I am a listed socialist, and whenever I am interested in politics. I have enjoyed reading mostly Shaw, Schopenhauer, Ibsen, Voltaire, Eugene O'Neill, Saroyan, Dos Passos and Thoreau.

Poets who have influenced me? Well, I am finally that kind of a poet who cannot do anything else but poetry. I like Keats. Poetry is another world. Poetry is the story of the soul. Poetry is the story of the psyche, Music is the sound of the soul. Painting is the picture of the soul. I like Verdi and Botticelli for music and painting. I am never a friend of war; I like William Morris and Wilfred Gibson.

"Didn't you ever search for another star?" and others. The psyche is free. Poetry is the story of the search for freedom. Poetry is the story of the psyche and its trials and jubilations.

Until recent years I have never been able to make up my mind about Thoreau. I have finally settled in a rooming house (The Walden House) in Montclair. Poetry is poor. Art is poor. The best things are never to be had for riches. I live on a budget of $80 a month. I cook my own meals. I live over a stove. This is a real good feed for a tramp who is used to that sort of thing. I am even contented.

SHIRLEY KAUFMAN

Born 1923, Seattle, Washington. Lived in San Francisco since marriage to Bernard Kaufman, Jr. We have three daughters. Attended U. of Washington. B.A. from UCLA, M.A. in English from San Francisco State College, 1967, guided by Mark Linenthal, Director of Poetry Center. Won Academy of American Poets prize at S. F. State. Read at the "Discovery" program of the YMHA Poetry Center in New York, 1967. Published in *Atlantic, Harper's, Kayak, The Nation, The New Yorker, Poetry,* many quarterlies.

Read poetry in high schools in and around San Francisco for Pegasus program of S. F. State College. Recently translated book by Israeli poet Abba Kovner (with Nurit Orchan) and will continue to translate contemporary Hebrew poetry, while writing my own poems.

I am lifted alternately by the voices of Williams and Roethke. Rilke has probably been the strongest influence. Lorca. Pound. And my teachers at S. F. State: Jack Gilbert, Robert Duncan, John Logan.

I write what comes, without looking around for it.

I write because I like to. Sometimes it even makes me happy.

I write because I feel something strongly, like the love/hate struggle of "Mothers, Daughters." Or the violence in Watts a few months after I saw the Watts Towers for the first time. But you can't make poems by shouting, "I feel!" Or collecting sensations. Need to discover the sound, the form, the "objects" of the experience. Mostly it begins with something irrational. There's a slow sinking of some intense experience where I can't get at it. And then—amazing—the poem begins. With everything else I've accumulated along the way.

I think poetry is a sort of organized irrationality. Like trying to become human. Or being a woman. And since there is no direct access to truths or meanings, I try to make some pattern out of observation, memory, fantasy—and the pain or joy I get from involvement with family, people and the physical world. Always the possibility that—at some rare interval—I'll see past what I know at the moment.

ERIC TORGERSEN

Born in Huntington, New York; twenty-six years old. Attended Cornell (1960–64) and Iowa Writers Workshop (1966–68), separated by two years in the Peace Corps in Ethiopia. Greatly indebted to two early writing teachers: Walter Slatoff and Baxter Hathaway.

I have until recently written poetry under the assumption that it was largely a matter of knowing (in detail) what to say; no more demanding set of rules has ever lasted more than a month or two. Thus, though "The Story of White Man Leading Viet Cong Patrol" is a found poem composed from a newspaper article, it was done not from any commitment to finding poems in the papers, but because the single occasion presented itself.

I now reject that old assumption, and in the future will insist on certain basic understandings. Like everyone else in this country, the poet has to fight constantly to keep his mind free; perhaps more than others he must fight to free his language, which is everywhere in chains.

WILLIAM HARMON

A 31-year-old native of Concord, N. C., now living in Deer Park, Ohio, and attending the University of Cincinnati as Elliston Fellow. A. B. Univ. of Chicago 1958, A. M. there 1968; another master's degree at Univ. of North Carolina, also 1968. Never studied writing as such under anybody, but my awareness of the scope of possibilities in literature was enormously increased at Chicago in the mid-50's by Prof. Norman Maclean, the best teacher I ever had. Everybody's everything influences my poetry; if I had to pin it down to a poet, then I'd have to say Pound. And, lately, Whitman.

I think about poetry all the time and write a great deal. Two years ago I began wanting to write a poem about my home town, and it was to be a poem called *Looms*, about the rise of the textile industry in the South from about 1880. But I found that the available materials—tradition, language, self, history, poetry—and all contexts were lacking for this simple-seeming undertaking, and I thought then that what I would have to do is write a series of long poems, eight or nine of them, to reconstitute the elements of the theater of my enterprise. The first part is "Treasury Holiday," a constitution dealing with my self in relation to a particular time. "My Big Chickadee," the second part, deals with my self in relation to others; it is a love poem that also concerns war and poetry. Part three is "William Tecumseh Sherman," hard going, getting at history through eloquence and spite, in Sherman, Stilwell, Mao, and other poet-generals. The fourth part, underway now, repeats certain themes already stated, with elaborations, so as to consolidate my position. Yet to come: "Religious Art of the Twenty-first Century," "Of Vulgar Eloquence" and "Looms" proper.

Aesthetic theories are wonderful but so hard to say. Poetry is a public phenomenon. It tries to register, in changed matter, the current energy without sacrificing too much of the virtue of energy to the facts of matter, such pernicious fictions as thought, feeling, plot, character, rhythm, expression, form. If that doesn't make sense, the topic itself is part of *Looms*. I hate to be gnomic, I want very very much to be absolutely clear about this, but I think almost all formulations of aesthetic are impossible. As a counterweight, I could say that everybody knows what poetry is; and they surely do.

Began June 4, 1937, in Santa Fe. WWII brought my family to Vallejo, California, where I grew slowly, cut school, duck-hunted, learned about girls, and cultivated a religion of loneliness, lying, and drawing: devotion thereto sustained me until conversion to poetry. Started Napa College at twenty-one and took a degree at San Francisco State where I now teach.

My teachers: Dad, who taught flycasting, what to watch for, wing-shooting, care—said No, and never wished to own anything he couldn't use in the woods; Mom, who dreamed of being a dancer, grew things everywhere, and said Yes; Albert T. Anderson, professor at SF State, who taught by example not to abandon those who falter (and his Mary, freed by love to laugh at his wake over the irony of a poet dying in a bank); Juanita, my wife; younger brother Mike who grew up first; of course John Logan; my sons Dylan and Colin (at this moment naked, running in dizzymaking circles).

Poets who influence me: Pascal terrified by the silence of those infinite spaces, Mother Goose, Thomas, Basho, Aeschylus, Anon. (& Hieronymus), Rilke, a deaf right ear, the Fool, e. e., Flaubert hammering on his cracked kettle, Bach, a broken left leg, Bruckner, Kollwitz, Hart Crane, Mandelstamm beating the woods for an axe handle for his executioner, Logan, Bartleby, Issa, Adam in Paradise naming the strange creatures—woman the only creation strange as his words.

Poetics: most of my writing done with a live inkpen in a Volkswagen parked where I can drink creole coffee from a thermos while light begins on the lake to disturb morning flights of duck. Although I burn to know how the artist does it, poems remain miraculous to me as snails, ineluctable as the iron flute. Poetry is not a craft but a necessity, like love. Poetry is for keeps.

I write to celebrate.

JOSEPH CARDARELLI

I was born on payday in West by God Virginia on Jan. 21, 1944. Conception that leads to real birth must have begun with a wild uncle who would not shave his hair or trim his toenails. Mountain people. Then in Washington, D.C., because of suburbs, parochial schools, and Walt Disney, conception was completed: with wine, loose women, and a life of petty crime at an early age. Ray Charles.

It's all about the indigenous blues music idiom of this region of America. It is the redemptive & at the same time incalculable human incident. It is also the demonic. It comes in a tradition or culture like a virus. Blues is why United States of America. It is all alive & right here & one must be touched by it before any of this may be touched. If one knows, soon it is part of one. Then one is part of it. Then one is it. Blues is one. Blues. My poems. That is what I am talking about. What I mean is please listen to people.

Quickly then, '55 Olds, dark-skinned girl, Rimbaud, bull bass, beat literature, Univ. of Md., Pound, Williams, speed, Rudd Fleming, Joe Giordano, a tall girl named Cathy, hashish, Davis, Mingus, B.S. Economics 1965. Marriage to Cathy, odd jobs, rediscover Rolling Stones & Beatles, to Hopkins Writing Seminars with Elliott Coleman. Pot, beer, horses' teeth, M.A. '67. A band right now with Jim my brother, named Paradise BeBop. Teaching too at Md. Inst. of Art. Right now I'm here in Baltimore but I won't be here long. 1969.

COLEMAN BARKS

32. Born and raised in Chattanooga, Tenn. Educated at the University of North Carolina and at Univ. of California at Berkeley. Taught for two years at Univ. of Southern California. Alvaro Cardona-Hine's workshop kept me writing on a regular basis while I was in Los Angeles. He was the one who got me interested in the powers of the short poem (*Body*). James Dickey's work also has been an influence (*Choosing*), and W. S. Merwin's. I am now with the English Dept. at the University of Georgia in Athens. I have been writing poetry fairly steadily for the last six years but only recently began to send some of it around to the little mags. (*Ann Arbor Review, Tennessee Poetry Journal, New, Chelsea, Kumquat,* etc.) A selection appears in the *New Generation of Poets* anthology (Black Sun Press, New York). The poetry I am working on now is very different from anything I've done before. Much less anecdotal.

I have a hard time trying to be serious about my "poetics." Everything I think to say sounds pretentious, or true for only a few poems, or plagiarized from Keats's letters. All I can say for sure is that the reasons and methods behind what I write are muddled, and derivative. And that an important part of my consciousness revives when I'm working on a poem, like when I take a good, much-needed nap in the middle of the afternoon. It seems true to think of the imagination relaxing at such times, with its face directly against the world, taking more and more deeply the print of the bedspread. Making of it finally a design that includes a particular ear, a cheek, a nose, a forehead. With poetry I would like to keep that pressure of images on the face and to walk out with it written all over me. Maybe so people will laugh and think they know me better because they've seen me just waking up.

SOPHIA CASTRO-LEON

I was born in Chicago, I am thirty-eight, and my parents emigrated from Greece. I have traveled and lived in various countries most of my life and consider this important in the development of my writing. In particular I cite having lived as a child in Greece and as an adult in Pakistan, where I had the opportunity to travel through much of India. My whole exposure to the Orient with trips to various countries I consider as very important.

I have studied at colleges in Chicago and California, at UCLA, where I attended poetry workshops, and in the workshop taught by Alvaro Cardona-Hine in Los Angeles.

I feel my work has been influenced by the Chinese poetry I have been able to read in translation and some of the Spanish, Greek, and American poetry. As to individual poets, I can't cite any particular influence. I feel I gained much from reading the work of James Wright, W. S. Merwin, Gary Snyder, Denise Levertov, and Rilke.

I live in the Los Angeles area. For the past year I have been studying Zen Buddhism with Zen Master Joshu Sasaki in Los Angeles.

Primarily these poems were written in terms of the struggle to go beyond the ego. They attempt the inner journey. The language I found I could best use for this was one of natural images. Through them I attempted an articulation of the inner search.

Thirty-one years old; born in Buffalo, N.Y.; degrees from Denison Univ. and the University of Iowa; studied writing under Paul Bennett at the former, at the latter Nelson Algren made the main impression; poets whose work has influenced—Shakespeare, Christ, Rembrandt, Wodehouse (P.G.), Kafka, Cummings, Williams, Dave Kelly, Fitzgerald, Hemingway, Fenton W. Dixon, Walt Disney probably Randolph Scott the Great Gildersleeve who knows . . .

Am presently writing in Buffalo.

A few years ago I decided poetry is "that way of feeling into words," and prose: "making something"—because I'd wondered for a time how to say the difference if someone ever asked. But now I don't know. Maybe poetry is what a guy hands you and says is poetry: if it's any good, then it's "good poetry." If it looks like prose because of being fat and having even left and right-hand margins and you say "that looks like prose to me" and he says "okay, it's prose," then it's prose. The point is does it sing or bite. I mean does something happen in your cells when you read or hear it. (Or rub it against your belly: let's leave the doors unlocked.) Because another way I sometimes think of it is "words on a piece of paper." To forget what Bly says or Dickey says or Creeley or (even) Williams said and read the thing as though it's early again and nothing's been defined yet: which of course is the case, and every poet knows not a single word in the language has ever been really used, not the way it was meant to and he will tonight or tomorrow or next week when the snow is due to melt or come.

That's how to come to it once it's written: how it gets there is something else. I need space and quiet, but sometimes I don't. Sometimes beer and TV, sometimes a bus ride. Whatever produces the condition of feeling—as opposed to fearing (which goes in, the opposite direction) or "thinking" or assuming an attitude—the condition of expanding across the borders of your skin:

> to stand fullblown and occupy
> your several rightful fields of air

so you can bring back and write what they contain.

When I wrote the five poems here I had other words for such matters, and by the time these appear will be somewhere else. The thing is to avoid absorbing too much of other men's—even writers', maybe especially writers'—realities, less of their "theories," to feel your own life. I suppose the best poet is more fully himself than others are theirs.

341

DAVID HILTON

Born in Oakland, California, in 1938, and grew up in a Bay Area typical suburb. B.A., San Jose State; Pfc, U. S. Army (pre-Vietnam); M.A., California State College at Hayward. As of now, a Ph.D. aspirant at the University of Wisconsin, Madison. I "learned" poetry mainly through writing it, revising it, talking about it with fellow poets, reading it copiously, trying out its different possibilities, writing it and revising it. I'm still learning of course; it doesn't stop. Two poets have been revelations to me. When I discovered the poetry of Theodore Roethke I felt as if I had never read a poem before. And later I found W. S. Merwin achieving things I did not think possible. My notion of what a poem is follows William Carlos Williams's definition, "A poem is a small (or large) machine made of words." A poem should be made, says Williams, "with such intensity of perception that it lives with an intrinsic movement of its own to verify its authenticity." This makes poems hard to write: no prescriptive forms into which you can "cast" your "material"; no comfortable symbolic structures through which your "material" takes on "significance." Form and structure *can* emerge, but only out of the energy of the perceptions. I try to make the image bear most of the burden of the poem's reality, to get, like, a green horse and a shriveled propeller to inhabit the same reality, the one which, by their relationship, they create. The perceptions need not be weird or surreal; see, e.g., the poems of Gary Snyder. Anything can *work*. That's what makes it difficult.

Born in Albany, N.Y., February 3, 1947. Raised in rural Hudson River Valley, now living elsewhere. Hamilton College ('64–'66); transferred to Antioch College ('66–'69), where I studied poetry under Judson Jerome. Influenced now by the ideas of the "deep" or subjective image. More specifically, Merwin's *The Lice*. Now spending most of my time writing and thinking while finishing studies.

Imagery controls my poems. Having discovered my vision lies on the shadow side, I am moving away from the "external" descriptive images (*Marina, Dead Wasp*) toward an imagery more deeply rooted in my own imagination (section I of *Things You Left Behind, I Will Give You a Purpose*).

Poetry can justify itself in at least three ways today: (1) as an explorer below the conscious mind, (2) as a social-political instrument, and (3) as an expression of love. The preceding statement is worthless as a dictum, but adequate enough as a "framework." I am drawn now to dream imagery in an attempt to capture the uncensored emotion or matrix of emotions which is as close as we can come to the truth. Not art as therapy, but the search for values leads inevitably inward.

Mary Ellen Solt was born in Gilmore City, Iowa, in 1920. She has studied at Iowa State Teachers College, the University of Iowa, and has participated in poetry workshops at Columbia, and the YMHA Poetry Center at New York. She has also studied at the School of Letters and in the Design Program at Indiana University. She currently lives in Bloomington, Indiana.

"The poets who have most influenced me are: William Carlos Williams, Louis Zukofsky, Ian Hamilton Finlay, and the Noigandres Group (Augusto de Campos, Haroldo de Campos, Decio Pignatari).

"I started out in the way of making poems to be learned from Williams and Zukofsky after I had done my stint with the poet-teachers. I wasn't too satisfied with the results. When I began making concrete poems in the spring of 1963, having been introduced to this new way of writing by Ian Hamilton Finlay, I began actually to make concrete poems, without really intending to, as I was studying a Brazilian anthology published by the Noigandres Group. When I made my first concrete poem, bad as it was, I knew that I had found the way of making poems most suited to my own needs. That is to say, when I use more traditional linear-grammatical-syntactical forms, I feel that I am being redundant in terms of what has been done over and over again by other and former poets. The forms of concrete poetry, which are unique to each poem, seem to permit me to express what I have to say in a way that belongs only to myself in the particular instance and to the tendencies toward highly concentrated, visual communication at work in the most advanced areas of thought in our time generally."

WILLIAM HATHAWAY

I was born in Madison, Wisconsin, December 18, 1944 and educated by the Ithaca Public Schools in Ithaca, N.Y. There were a couple of separate years in Rome and Switzerland but nobody was particularly enthusiastic about my several talents. Freshman year at the American College in Paris and then on to Cornell University, where they felt I'd be "happier somewhere else" due to a failure to pass geology. So I did the exciting things you read about on book jackets until the Pentagon became too bothersome. At the University of Montana I found a congenial atmosphere, my wife, and Richard Hugo, who is a fine poet and an excellent poetry teacher. I am presently at the Iowa Writer's Workshop.

I try to avoid saying anything definite about my personal "theory of poetics." I feel that academic *and* non-academic poets take poetics too seriously. Perhaps what would please me most would be more discussion of poems and less of poetry. All poets write good and bad poems. Obviously if the poem fails to generate enthusiasm in the poet during its creation it has failed its most important function. As for the audience of a poem, they either like it, dislike it, or are indifferent. To my mind the worst poems are boring poems. Personally I have a hard time finishing a short Wallace Stevens poem but I know poets whose own work fascinates me who can't leave Stevens alone. I won't fight to the death over Stevens' right to write poems but I will squeak out the notion that pedantry and esoterism have no place in the reading of poems. For me poetry is like skiing, it can or cannot be competitive but it is always exhilarating. I find writing poems cheaper and in many ways more hazardous.

345

Age: 25; born in New York City (grew up in Cleveland, Ohio); B.A. from Oberlin College (in studio art), and an M.F.A. from The University of Iowa; worked with David Young at Oberlin, Marvin Bell, Anselm Hollo, and Ted Berrigan at The U of I; influences: Stevens, Bly, Merwin, Koch, Ashbery, O'Hara.

I am reminded of Craig Breedlove and of the many times he has attempted to break the land speed record at the Bonneville Salt Flats (sometimes successfully). One try landed him in an 18-foot deep pool of brine; he was able to walk away from the wreckage. Not everyone is so lucky. I've always wanted to step out of a car traveling at, say, 600 mph (the car, incidentally, is shaking apart, disintegrating) and walk over to the stands where I would enjoy a Pepsi and talk to an incredibly beautiful woman.

RAYMOND DIPALMA

Born: September 27, 1943. New Kensington, Pennsylvania
Educ: B.A. Duquesne University, 1966. M.F.A. University of Iowa,
    1968
Presently: Instructor in Creative Writing, Bowling Green University,
    Bowling Green, Ohio
Studied Under: Marvin Bell, George Starbuck, Anselm Hollo
Influences: John Ashbery, Djuna Barnes
Statement on Poetics: These two collaborative poems were written
    about cities we had never visited. We took turns writing
    lines till we had fourteen. This made it a sonnet, we thought.

    The continuously changing nature of my poetry would make
    any formal statement ridiculous. Writing these collaborations
    refreshed the changes.

    (The first paragraph of this "statement" was written
    by Steve Shrader and me with Steve sitting at the typewriter
    and me sitting on a couch to his right facing in the opposite
    direction. I wrote the second paragraph and the third alone,
    and at different times).

luke (joseph brown, sj)

My Life. I was born in st. louis in 1944. i started writing at age 11. in 1962 i entered the society of jesus. the stages of my writing have been guided by three men: leonard waters, sj (who told me what i couldn't say); john knoepfle (who showed me the smallest number of words necessary); elliot coleman (who helped me ascertain whether or not i had said what i intended). the undergraduate journey was between Marquette U. and St. Louis U. i then studied at the writing seminars at johns hopkins.

my influences. ogden nash, t. s. eliot, thomas merton.

poetry. for me, the stuff of poetry is the paradox and the mystery of human experience. to be honest and true. to see things clearly. i admit my individual viewpoint. because i am black (or light brown, to be exact) i am drawn to the endured suffering in this world. the lonely songs uttered in man's "unattended moment" i want to hear and put down. because i am a christian, i believe that absurdity can be a positive condition of humanity—a starting point for choice. i try to recognize all of the possibilities of man. he suffers: loves: laughs: questions: endures. to know as many approaches to this mystery and paradox of reality as can be discovered and explored: my reason for writing. my poetry is signed "luke" because that gospel and the traditions of its writer seem to express most of my ramblings toward definition and identity. poetry keeps me alive.

I write poetry because I can and because I know the poet's secret, that he is happy. However exasperated by his place as an appendage of his culture and troubled by paranoia and addiction, when he is swimming in that flood of images or thigh deep in the fecund earth of prophecy he is the first, beloved child.

These poems are the inchoate products of my apprenticeship and it is hard to say much about them. If they reveal any influences I hope it is of those I admire such as good father Williams and mother Ginsberg.

The Home is an actual place in Brooklyn in which I lived for three years during my early teens. It is a love poem, written out of isolation and shyness but it is also a poem of revenge. I first took up words as a weapon; as many of us, I was raised in an atmosphere of war.

Chameleon I brought up blindly from some place inside that knew better than (what I called) myself, what was going on. It is a poem of personal exploration, and started as a blur of sound below my mind.

Last winter, while studying with John Logan, I wrote the poem *Snips and Snails*. It is one of several poems distilled from the juice of this city: this big, overripe apple full of so many people who are ready but have no place to go.

Other particulars might include: age, twenty-five; place of birth, Brooklyn; and present home, the Lower East Side; other teachers and mentors Diane Wakoski and Harriet Sohmers Zwerling.

As for the future, I would like to find an alternative to the poetry of individual sensibility; to move in the direction of chants and rituals and do with words what the L.T. does in *Paradise Now*.

STUART PETERFREUND

Stuart Peterfreund, 24, was born in Brooklyn, New York. He has studied at Cornell University, the University of California at Irvine, and is currently at the University of Washington. He lists as major influences on his writing: Theodore Roethke, Robert Creeley, John Berryman, Alfred Starr Hamilton, Douglas Eichhorn, Robert Sward, David Ray, James Wright, Donald Justice, Dennis Saleh, Robert L. Jones, and Louis Simpson.

"It seems to me that the best poets of the younger American School (40 and over, recent corpses allowed) such as Berryman, Logan, Merwin, Justice, Simpson and Roethke, are men, who having acknowledged the raw deal they got by being born (something Lowell has never gotten over), have made of the world a positive, though not necessarily optimistic vision, which they have justified by somehow withdrawing from the darkness and allowing themselves to be reborn into their own, visionary worlds. And when I speak of visionary, I don't mean mystical, I mean metaphorical. And it is easier to live in the metaphor than in the darkness, as well as being far more productive. The projectivists, the New York poets, the *kayak* surrealists all fail for me because they never make the value judgment necessary in the creation of the metaphor for darkness. They show, instead, how science can kill poetry: by recording process without questioning significance, by stressing the 'how' without questioning the 'why.'

"At any rate, in my own writing, I find it necessary to control a reality. And the only reality I can control is the one I make for *me*. It's not the most exciting of all worlds. It's memories of my mother and grandfathers, the few girls I have loved, good friends I get drunk and riot with every time I see them, the several times we ruled the world. It's sitting and drinking wine, listening to classical music on the radio very late at night in New York, knowing that I'm alive. It's stumbling through the dark and loving it for a minute, the way you love a city you've visited because you know your way around. And in the dark, if you can find your way, you're doing all right. There are many ways to do it, the best of them being to sing.

THOMAS HANNA

Age: 28
Home: born in Utica, New York; now living in Chipiona, Spain.
Education: Cornell University and University of Buffalo.
Influences: David Ray has influenced my work, but his poems haven't. His poems have affected my life. If you mean yesterday, Shakespeare, Poe, Tu Fu, the Iroquois, the Maori. I hope to pay them off sometime.
Currently: I am trying the poetry hustle, but plan to change my line of work.

BARBARA L. GREENBERG

Born Barbara Levenson on August 27, 1932, in Boston; live now in a Boston suburb with surgeon husband and two sons. Was graduated from Wellesley College in 1953, during the era of heady T. S. Eliot study, but Poe, Longfellow and Whitman (the best-loved poets of my grammar school days) have had, I think, the greater influence on my own poetry.

While not opposed to experiment of any kind, I do feel that words, with their accumulated power of meaning and magic, are still the substance of poetry, and that insight is the impulse behind it. Thus, I am suspicious of what is easy or accidental in wording, in form, or in content. I think, too, that the traditional forms (e.g., the sestina), far from being irrelevant in our time, still offer a vigorous challenge to the poet willing to work at them. If the impulse behind the poem is genuine, discipline will not destroy, but, rather, refine it.

DON SHEA

I am 29, was born in New York City, and have studied poetry under M. L. Rosenthal at N.Y.U. As to poets who have influenced me, the problem is that the work is as much the computer's as it is mine. To prepare vocabulary data for the program, I had to address myself to the question: What constitutes a poetic vocabulary? I could find no satisfactory theoretical guidelines here, so I chose what seemed to me a fairly eclectic group of poems and built from them a vocabulary of roughly 2000 words—the poets included Dylan Thomas, Yeats, Jeffers, Robert Lowell, Frost, Stephens, Williams, Pound, Eliot, and Cummings.

The poems presented here were written by an IBM 360 computer. They represent a partial selection from more than 1500 stanzas, and are unaltered with the exception of punctuation. The computer was programmed to assemble and print common grammatical structures in a variety of verse forms. A random mixture of punched cards was used as input, containing words with syntactic codes, and in some cases codes indicating tense and number. The words themselves were chosen from a sampling of poems by the above named poets.

I find no objection to the reasoning that the response to an excellent poem in a book of verse is the response to some mood or condition, uniquely human, that is expressed with a particular urgency, grace, or evocative power. But I think it should be emphasized the method of evoking the response is purely abstract. A word or sentence spoken face to face is a total physiological expression, replete with gesture and intonation, while a word or combination of words on a printed page is a very different thing. In any case, the question of meaning must be distinguished from the question of genesis; intelligibility, at whatever level, does not depend upon "human" production. It depends upon human interpretation. The question is not how what we read was written, but rather, how we understand and respond to what we read.

353

Age (as of October 1969) 26. Born Dallas, Texas. Moved with wife Anne to San Francisco in 1962. Presently living in Berkeley, California. Studied literature and creative writing at North Texas State University, University of San Francisco, San Francisco State College, and University of California at Berkeley. Took creative writing courses under Robert Duncan, John Logan and William Dickey. Influential poets include: Levertov, Tu Fu, Whitman, Blake, Roethke, Stein, Pound. I am presently an Assistant Professor of Creative Writing at San Francisco State College engaged in an educational revolution in favor of new definitions of learning and opposed to an archaic and monarchial political Trusteeship. Also I am the Assistant Director of the Poetry Center at San Francisco State College.

I believe poems are metaphorical statements about human consciousness. My best poems are written about feelings that confuse or trouble me. My worst poems are word-games written about words and about what words can do. When a poem clicks for me I will rework it until it feels whole. It feels "whole" when it has about it all the coherence, mystery, ambiguity and sensuous rhythms which I associate with any Living Thing. I crave a passionate lucidity. To be lucid without passion is a bore to write, and to be passionate without a ferocious clarity is a bore to read. Every gesture of my daily life is the subject matter for poetry but sometimes I am dumb and closed and cannot see the meanings around me. Metaphysically a poem for me is a sort of shrine whose symbolic forms praise the meaningfulness of all things; physically it is a block of language which feels good in the brain above and slightly behind my eyes. I write at night. All poetry proceeds from the Body.

FLOYCE ALEXANDER

Most of my life has been spent in the provinces. I was born in Fort Smith, Arkansas, grew up in Wellington, Kansas, and Granger, Washington, and now live in Pullman, Washington. All small towns except for five years in Seattle and return-ticket journeys to New Orleans, Mexico City, Los Angeles, and San Francisco.

On 7 May, 1969, I was married with Paula Joy Thornton.

On December 31, 1968, I turned 30. For six years I've worked as an editor for Washington State University Press. I have a B.A. from the University of Washington where I met Theodore Roethke and David Wagoner, among other writers. I began writing poems out-of-school and taking them to Roethke. He encouraged me to continue.

Among my elders I admire the work of Gary Snyder, James Wright, John Logan, Robert Creeley, W. S. Merwin, Galway Kinnell, René Char, and Andrei Voznesensky. Of the dead I continue to read Whitman, Hart Crane, Kafka, Blake, Cesar Vallejo, and Johannes Bobrowski. I don't even know how much I've learned from teachers of the soul: Robert Bly, Howard McCord, and Betty Ludington, sculptor, painter, potter, weaver.

If I am to see as much of the universe as I can, I must become capable of seeing through my own senses. The way I hear, and however I may touch, smell, or taste, this world provides the poem with its skeleton, as the eyes give it its marrow. The secret of the poem is balance, suspension of consciousness between mental clarity and imaginative density.

Nowhere deals with a kind of utopia where the spirit is created in a moment of fusion between human and inhuman roots. The same process occurs in *Poem for a Painter*, but the presence of the Vietnam war and the young painter, ravaged by that war, make the poem more a lamentation than a celebration. *Aphrodite* hovers between sadness and joy: perhaps nostalgia gives the poem its balance.

The Lotus Eaters was written the day after King's murder, in a state of outrage which connected the immediacy of the event with my own Southern ancestry. *Li Po*, composed two months later, evokes a nostalgia similar to *Aphrodite* in its content, though the form has mellowed in the two years separating those poems. *Guerrilla* tries to bring together two questions: How are humans to receive the most fundamental necessities of life? Is love—deep, rich love—possible in a world where plunder is accepted and rape encouraged through the apathy of the comfortable?

ROCHELLE RATNER

Born December 1948 in Atlantic City, N.J., and still living there. I began taking poetry seriously at age twelve and have been attempting to study it on my own ever since. In the winter of 1968, I received encouragement from A. R. Ammons and studied at Bread Loaf Writers' Conference the following summer.

It seems as if words on the page are pleading to become a language of silence. I'm plagued by emotions, and forever searching for new images to describe or defend them. Thus, each word that finds its way into the poem is a tight construction with many different meanings. I try to keep the poem as short as possible—hoping the careful reader will discover as much joy, if not *more*, in the things left unsaid.

The only form I include in poems is the one that best describes the moment of composition. In poems such as *The Maiden*, what might appear to have been a planned format was almost completely accidental. This is how it *should* be.

356

WILLIAM WITHERUP

Born in Kansas City, Missouri, on March 24, 1935. Currently living in San Francisco. Have done at least one quarter at the following institutions: Willamette University; The University of Washington; the University of Oregon; the University of Maryland Overseas Extension and San Francisco State College. Have studied under Ted Roethke and James B. Hall. Am currently employed as a warehouseman.

Poets who have had the greatest influence on my work are Theodore Roethke, Robert Bly, Rainer Maria Rilke, Federico Garcia Lorca, Pablo Neruda, Enrique Lihn, Nicanor Parra and most recently Alejandro Romualdo.

The poem comes out of silence, out of the creative matrix at the center of each of us. With me the poem usually begins with an embryonic image in the womb of the unconscious. The writing of the poem is the bringing to birth of the nascent image. In the process, as the image takes more definite form, it draws other images to it and this cluster of images finds its own rhythm as syntax. Generally, the germinating image is the strongest image in the poem. It is the central energy. On the Death of Theodore Roethke and Marian at Tassajara Springs are good examples. They both end with powerful images, images that I was only partly aware of, that I was pregnant with, that cried for birth, that glimmered in the unconscious night but that gradually took precise form in the patient labor of composition. The true poem is as much a discovery for the poet as it is for the reader.

As for that Waterloo of literary criticism, prosody or rhythm, I believe quite simply that you have to have a good ear. As the image rises out of silence, so does rhythm. The verbal texture exists in counterpoint to the silence surrounding it. I often think of the white space of the page that engulfs the poem as a visual metaphor of this silence. Some of my poems begin out of a need to give form to a rhythmic emotion that in the beginning has no imagery in mind. I am merely carried forward into the poem by an unconscious vocal gestus. Hybrid Villanelle on a Line of Li Po is one such poem; begun merely in response to my reading of a Li Po poem.

Poetry is language at its most physical. American poetry is American language at its most physical, as distinct from British English. I feel a good poem in my whole body. Often during composition I move around a lot. Though I do not listen to music when I write, I often feel like breaking into a rock dance. Then I know that a true poem is working, that I am not forcing it.

357

EDGAR PAIEWONSKY

I was born in the Dominican Republic; grew up there; then moved to Uruguay; then Peru. Finished high school in St. Thomas, Virgin Islands. There I began to read and write English poetry. One year at the University of Puerto Rico—my writing was helped by Prof. Marion Cumpiano. Later, at N.Y.U., I worked under Robert Hazel and M. L. Rosenthal. I'm now teaching at Fordham University, Department of Modern Languages. I'm twenty-six and married. My favorite poets are Machado, Vallejo, Paz, Eliot, Williams, Roethke, Michaux. Concretism has clearly influenced me.

For the last year I've been involved almost exclusively with *Icons*. This anthology presents a selection—articulated in a meaningful sequence. The reader should remember that each segment was originally written on a separate card, as a unit in itself. This allowed me to shuffle the cards freely, often arriving at combinations that would trigger off new icons. I have attempted to read the physical world as a map of my own self. In each of these pieces I've tried to isolate a mountain and a valley on this map. The detail, I believe, reveals the mechanism that underlies the whole. Essences are physical: the sperm; the egg; their fusion.

The correspondence between myself and the world has led me to reject metaphor or any other poetic device. The only "metaphor" in these *Icons* is the word EYES because it functions as an illustration of the formula that follows it.

Icons has been emerging slowly. I think of it as the record of my own personal quest. I believe it will increasingly depend on both words and visual symbols to communicate its meaning.

Age, 24. Born, Kendallville, Indiana. Moved soon after to Ocala, Florida, and later Paducah, Kentucky, where my family lived most of my life. Attended Oberlin College: B.A. in English literature, 1968. Robert Ober and I shared the same house on and off while undergraduates, and I think I learned the most about writing from the explorations we were each making during that time and the discussions we had about them. Robert Bly also offered valuable criticism. My sister (who looks like the actress Julie Christie) gave early encouragement to my interest in being an artist. The woods and lakes around my home contributed much to the sense of proportion I try to hold in mind toward most things that fascinate me. I could not have written recent poems without the presence of Kennette, who is wonderful and has shared everything.

Early poems were influenced by Robert Bly, James Wright, and Galway Kinnell. Recent work (written since the poems were chosen for this book) has been influenced by the poems of Gary Snyder and James Koller, and bears little resemblance to the poems printed here. Formal poetics usually bore me. Intra-specific aggression exists between poets, and anthologies of established poets read like ecological surveys: Black Mountain, San Francisco Renaissance, *Sixties* poets and *Kayak* poets, academics East & West. With cross-breeding and in some cases cross-pollination. Poets of the generation of '62 offered us the Apocalypse, filing two by two into the Surrealist Ark. The Eastern mind, symbolized by the drifting small boat, is hardly so categorical, divisive, and desperate. A sense of Unity in all things replaces a sense of moral superiority. Political commitment need not rigidify poetic explorations. For these reasons I try to avoid being a poetician. Pablo Neruda wrote without theories, though this fact has been subverted into a rigid dogma of the image. Neruda kept himself free of literary polemic and adapted to the best explorations of each new generation of poets, most often exceeding their efforts. In American poetry, only the range of Gary Snyder's poems attests to an equal energy and independence.

One last note: The half-time announcer at the 1969 Superbowl football game gave us this to consider: "The band will now execute the traditional designs and symbols of our national heritage." As a one-man band, I try to accomplish the same thing in my poems. There is no nourishment in our present Daley bread.

359

Age 25; born Washington, D.C.; present residence Fredericksburg, Virginia; B.A. Colgate University, M.A. Johns Hopkins University. I have studied writing under Bruce Berlind at Colgate and Elliott Coleman at Johns Hopkins; the former tried to teach me discipline and scruples, with the latter I began to hear a voluble silence and to understand the religiousness of words. My present occupation is Instructor of English at Mary Washington College.

What I am trying to do in my poetry is to confront the world as it sits in my backyard and in the back of my head; I am trying to understand it, bringing to it my own biases and complaints, to speak to it and more importantly, to listen. Sometimes this encounter fails to come off; it gets myopic, mischievous or merely zany—the ego-mania of things overpowers my words. Other times my words are able to free themselves, both from the sticky world and from a sticky me, to explore in their naïve resonances the distances. But this is still in my poetry an urge that has yet to fulfill itself; most of the time I'm simply trying to get close enough to hear.

Born 38 years ago in Brussels, Belgium, and brought up in a Catholic home for children. (My mother language is French but the mothering has ceased.) I now live in the middle of New York City with my husband, and teach English to Spanish ladies in the Anti-Poverty Program. Once took a course with Denise Levertov, whose influence like a distant wave was slow to come but strong and deep when it arrived. Touched "zero in the bone" with Emily Dickinson and journeyed in the warmer, more luxuriant zones of Wallace Stevens. Both these poets helped form my rhythm's early landscape.

Sound is crucial to my poems—assonance, internal rhymes, alliteration—and I like repeated tones as "lemur" and "summer," "river" and "water," in *Unaware That Avessek* . . . , a poem inspired by a geological map of Passadumkeag, Maine. I tend to be frugal with adjectives, and enjoy the spring-lock tightness of texture that sometimes results in using one-syllable end-line words. See "house," "smoke," "roast," "love," "things," and "grips" in the first three stanzas of *Force of Snow*. And there is also a feeling in my work for muscular verbs: "grip," "scrape," "crash," and "triggers" . . .

The Woman Who Loved Worms, my longest poem, began with a nagging but common enough vision of a butterfly. Some years before I had read of an 11th-century Japanese woman, who, defying the customs of her times, experimented with weevils and worms; she was looking for the principles underlying beauty. It took two years for the poem to shape itself in my unconscious terrain, but once full-fledged, I had only to listen, that is, to engage in a kind of divine attention, for the poem to be written.

But most of my other poems arrive piecemeal, sometimes with a first line, other times with only one word, even an ordinary one which the moment has made fresh and full of new perceptions. For example, *Force of Snow* began with the word "ordeal" (I later wrenched it out), and that solitary word haunted me for days until I put it down on paper. Also, unlike some poets, titles come easily to me, and they will in time demand a poem to look down on. An instance: the name *Cold Waltzes* danced in my mind months before I seized the first line of the poem.

The first drafts of my poems are often overcrowded with images, and like a ruthless landlord, I force myself to evict lines—even lines I like as "nightstick wind" in the original *Slumnight*. But to get the spareness and single metaphor of the first two stanzas, I had to rid the poem of every lax and unnecessary phrase.

I love poetry and cannot think of any life without it.

361

WILLIAM BROWN

A native of Los Angeles, William Brown attended Calvin College and the Iowa Writers' Workshop. He spent two years in Europe and now lives in New York City, where he makes his living as a freelance writer and editor. He is thirty.

"I would like to work out a 'poetics'—that is, I would like to know what I'm doing when I write. This would enable me, I think, to write poems very much different from the ones printed here. I imagine these future poems as fuller, longer and earthier. I am trying, in short, to write like Shakespeare, and I hope that some of my contemporaries will do the same. It would make things much more interesting than they are now."

I was born in San Francisco in 1942, during a war that's being forgotten: A.B. Berkeley, Ph.D. University of Washington. In classes, Jo Miles, Thom Gunn, John Logan encouraged me, but it was Ginsberg's *Howl* in 1956 that first made me think writers said anything, and it was Wayne Burns at U.W. who helped me understand what I was doing. Now I teach English at San Diego State College. It's sunny here.

I go on writing, not knowing why, though I have an idea of what writing is: discovering what it's like, or would be like, to be alive—a discovery always in some sense against the law, because you're supposed to stay dumb. We hear a lot about "technique" and "form" lately, how a piece of art is supposed to "work." That's all just a sophisticated form of censorship, a way of keeping one's eyes averted from the content, the vision.

When I write something, more and more I feel someone is going to take revenge on me for doing it. A few years ago I still had charm, when I wrote that Berkeley-sunglass-*Hudson Review* poem. But now what I do makes people increasingly disgusted, increasingly alarmed, especially if it's in prose, since people don't take poetry so seriously. Even so, my Malcolm X poem never made me many friends —white or black. I suppose because it has a little feeling in it for him, jerk that he was to get killed. Saying anything at all is getting risky, let alone writing. I can't think of much else to do while waiting, though. I'll see how the novel hits, my *Little Girl Lost*. I suppose that the worst that can happen is to have my vision dismissed as personal gloominess, to be told to cheer up and go swimming.

La Jolla really has a beautiful beach. You can swim in the ocean even during the winter.

It isn't enough.

DAN GILLESPIE

Age, thirty. Born in Ardmore, Oklahoma. I've lived and worked in many areas in the western states, but most of my life spent in Utah. I've worked continuously from the age of sixteen, taking my education in spare time, ranch hand, truck driver, construction, assembly lines, lumberyards, warehouses, reluctant soldier, etc. Attended the University of Utah over a period of eight years, on and off, English, philosophy, social sciences. No advanced degrees. My work in English did not include "creative writing." Currently living in Midvale, Utah, working as a warehouseman.

Influences on my work: James Wright, A. R. Ammons, Galway Kinnel, John Haines. I try to write poetry that is simple, stripped, direct, and felt; poetry that speaks in straightforward communication. My poems reflect my social and cultural preoccupations: a regional bias (the mountain West), a personal search for roots and a sense of tradition (historical Mormonism), and a deep-felt distrust for the social and technological currents of this country. The man who has seen Los Angeles has seen the future.

My poems are invariably "about something." That is, they are attempts at poetic statements, rather than artistic-intellectual word games, which, however much they may attract and amuse, rarely move the reader to an act of self-recognition or emotional response.

The poems in this book, hopefully, stand on their own, and should be understood on first reading without the need for "critical interpretation." The poems should reach out and touch, not mystify. I hope they have done so.

I was born in Buffalo, New York, in October 1940, but I spent most of my life in New England. For five years I lived in California —two of those years at Stanford, where I studied literature with Yvor Winters and Frank O'Connor and took a writing course from Malcolm Cowley. After that I dropped out of college and never went back. Instead I had jobs and wrote pulp paperbacks for extra money.

I don't know which poets have influenced me as well as the poets whose work I like. Among Americans, Dickinson, Stevens, Williams, Berryman, Lowell, and Plath. The writer who has influenced me the most is Edward Dahlberg, not only for his own work, but for the works of writers he revealed to me—including Juvenal, Aristotle and Darwin. Their work was so remote to this civilization and this culture (and so relevant), I began to uncover what was unique in the American language, what is honest in its tone and musical in its rhythms and sounds.

I have no particular credo where poetry goes; only that the heart is still the best judge of a good poem. To write a clumsy poem that is honest is better (and more rare) than to write a smooth poem that is a lie. In the three poems printed here I have tried to supply each with a content (style) that relates to the style (content) of the poem.

At present I live in Marblehead, Mass., with my husband. I teach poetry at Tufts University and published a book of novellas and stories with Houghton-Mifflin in October.

Age 26, born August 15, 1943. Spent first 20 years living on and around my father's wheat farm in north-central Montana. Took a degree in English from a small Montana teacher's college. Worked as a farm laborer and RR telegrapher. Went to Michigan State U. for graduate degree in American literature and quit. Joined the Merchant Marines and quit. Tried editing a little magazine and quit. Bummed off my friends while deciding what to do next. Now at University of California at Irvine working for an M.F.A. degree in creative writing.

I started writing when I was about 19. Kept at it without a real sense of commitment until I was 23 or so. Which is just about the time I gave up on graduate school, threw out my old poems and started over. Greatest help and biggest influence was my brother Rick, who, with the patience of a priest, read every poem I ever wrote.

DENIS JOHNSON

At the moment I am married with one child. So far the only college I have attended is the U of Iowa, where I am now an undergraduate. I have studied writing here under John Morgan and George Chambers, two poets who have very recently appeared, and under George Starbuck and Marvin Bell, both of whom have been around for a while. I was born in Munich, Germany, in July 1949.

"Things seem to become more clear when I write them down" is about as close as I can get to a statement of poetics. *Quickly Aging Here* and *Checking the Traps* are two poems which are born directly from this sentiment. The latter poem was the beginning of a minor obsession I had for syncopating two concerns of the poem within what I hoped was a coherent whole. The poem about baseballs was the culmination of this experiment. My only syllabic poem to date is *In a Rented Room*. I was interested in seeing how long and unvaried I could make the lines before the poem began to sag under their weight. Probably my favorite out of this five is *The Man Among the Seals*. It came from nowhere in particular, which seems to be a good place for poems to come from.

INDEX OF FIRST LINES